Peace
versus
POWER
in the Family

ABRAHAM A. LOW
Founder of Recovery, Inc.

Peace

versus
POWER
in the Family

Domestic Discord and Emotional Distress

Abraham A. Low, M.D.

Author of "Mental Health Through Will-Training"

Founder of Recovery, Inc.

Previously titled: Lectures to Relatives of Former Patients

WILLETT PUBLISHING CO.

Winnetka, Illinois

To the Patients of Recovery
who had the courage and dedication
to fulfill Dr. Low's plan for them

TABLE OF CONTENTS

PREFACE

"Peace Versus Power in the Family" offers a systematic philosophy of family harmony which can be used successfully by any family. For that reason, we have changed the title to better reflect the contents of the book. The philosophy of "Peace Versus Power in the Family" extends far beyond both the barriers of timeliness and the realm of psychiatry, setting forth techniques to implement that philosophy.

"Peace Versus Power in the Family" is offered in the belief that the family environment remains a powerful factor in the healthy functioning of the mind. The reader will find here a comprehensive system for understanding and controlling the forces at work in the domestic environment. Many people who want domestic harmony lack the means to achieve it. By reading these pages and grasping the essence of Dr. Low's message, "Peace Versus Power in the Family" can be a vital first step in achieving the domestic harmony so often sought and seldom reached.

This book was written under a particular set of conditions by a man of special background. In the early 1940's, commitment to a mental hospital was virtually the only remedy for mental illness; psychological definitions of mental disturbance were less subtle than they are today. Neither the recovering psychiatric patient nor the surrounding family had any guidance for establishing an environment conducive to mental health.

To give the reader an historical perspective, the lectures contained in this book were given by the author between 1938 and 1941, the first and third Sunday of each month, before audiences composed mainly of relatives of patients at the Psychiatric Institute of the University of Illinois Medical School. Each of the lectures was presented in several installments, covering two to four months.

When the Recovery group left the Illinois Research Hospital in 1941 to become an independent lay-organization, lectures to the relatives ceased. Recovery, Inc., asked Dr. Low to publish this valuable material, and in 1943 this was done in the form of a paperback photo-lift edition of limited quantity. Subsequently, Dr. Low's book, "Mental Health Through Will-Training"* was published.

Following Dr. Low's death in 1954, Recovery, Inc., continued with the self-help method developed by Dr. Low for this lay-organization. In the years since, its phenomenal growth in size and strength has proved the validity of the method and developed a vast new interest in Dr. Low's other work. In answer to this widespread demand, "Lectures to Relatives of Former Patients" was republished in more permanent form by Mae W. Low in 1966.

The following pages are as the author wrote them, with only minor changes taken from Dr. Low's original notes.

Phyllis Low Cameron
Marilyn Low Schmitt
Chicago, 1984

*Originally published by The Christopher Publishing House, Boston, Mass. Currently available through Willett Publishing Co., Winnetka, IL.

INTRODUCTION

Psychiatric after-care has for its objective the prevention of relapses. It may be assumed with reasonable safety that the same set of circumstances which caused the original breakdown is also responsible for the subsequent relapse. To prevent relapses then means to gain adequate control of these circumstances.

Chief among the disturbing circumstances is the emotional situation in the domestic scene. When the patient returns from the hospital he is received into an atmosphere which is charged with anxious expectation. The relatives, wife, husband, father, mother—are eager, solicitous, protective. But their eagerness is overdone, and the solicitude and protectiveness assume all too easily the mark of apprehensive fitfulness. The ex-patient is watched, cautioned, superintended, directed and interfered with. The unceasing supervision suggests to him that the reality of his recovery is not trusted—once mentally ill, always mentally ill. The stigma of mental disease rears its ugly head and stares him in his perplexed face.

If the ex-patient rebels, insisting on a measure of free movement and self-directed action, he is likely to be reminded that he has to "take it easy," that he is still "nervous" and in need of "lots of rest." With subtle reminders of this kind the fact is painfully accentuated that although discharged he is still on probation; once mentally ill, always mentally ill. The home situation is now heavy with the spirit of the stigma.

The ex-patient may continue his rebellion. He rejects insinuations and provokes arguments. The more he resists the "well meant" advice the more rigid becomes the supervision. A vicious cycle ensues. The determined resistance offered by the patient—the "parolee"—causes the relatives to intensify their pressure, and the increased pressure provokes more determined resistance. Tempers explode and nerves snap. In the end, a violent outburst occurs, and the patient is hustled back to the hospital. There the fact of a relapse is entered upon the record and the time-honored dictum of "once mentally ill, always mentally ill" is confirmed, verified and perpetuated.

This is not an attempt to incriminate domestic discord as the sole source of relapses. Nor is the author sufficiently naive to consider all relapses as preventable. There can be no doubt, however, that the temperamental explosions of an ill-balanced domestic scene are currently producing readmissions which could be avoided if tempers were adequately curbed. To express it otherwise: unbridled tempers are closely correlated with the mounting rate of recurrences. Conversely, an effective curb on domestic temper can be expected to reduce the incidence of relapses.

The explanatory remarks appended to most of the lectures are primarily meant to serve as guides to physicians.

Peace

versus

POWER

in the Family

ENVIRONMENTAL IRRITATION AND
INDIVIDUAL RESISTANCE

If a patient, after finishing a course of treatment, is pronounced recovered he is sent home. That does not mean that he needs no further care. It merely means that he is no longer in need of hospital care. The hospital has done its share by supplying treatment. Now the home must do its part by providing after-treatment.

There are two types of patients. The one is easily wounded, ruffled and upset; the other is of a coarser fiber and relatively immune to irritations. We shall call the one the relatively vulnerable, the other the relatively impregnable. The latter requires no after-care; the former is in dire need of it. But mark it: except for clear-cut instances you do not know beforehand whether your son, husband, sister or father belongs to the more vulnerable or to the more impregnable variety. Since you cannot predict to which group your relative belongs you must be prepared to provide for after-care should it be required.

If a patient is sent home he returns to the environment in which his health broke prior to his admission to the hospital. The question may be raised whether when he broke, the family environment was partly or largely responsible for the break. If so, that environment may break him again. You see how vitally important is the influence of home environment.

Environmental Factors Alone Do Not Explain Mental Breakdowns

It will be necessary for you to know something about the relationship between environment and individual particularly with regard to mental breakdowns. Undoubtedly when your son or husband broke, you asked the painful question, "Why in the world did he have to break?" Your answer most likely ran in the customary channels. You surmised that the girl whom your son courted disappointed his expectations, or that the strain of preparing for a final examination drained his feeble energies, or that business reverses, with the attendant brooding, helped to cloud your husband's mind. Explanations of this kind place the blame on environment. The girl and final examinations and the business reverses are all environmental circumstances. When you engaged in this line of reasoning, you forgot to consider that, after all, millions of people suffer disappointments in love, failure in examinations, losses in business without experiencing a mental break. Obviously, environment alone is not sufficient to account for mental disease. Another factor must be considered—that factor is constitution.

Varieties of Environments and Individuals

Briefly, environment may have a minimal, average, or excessive amount of irritation. Similarly, an individual's constitution may be endowed with a minimal, average, or excessive measure of resistance. Figure 1 (page 17) illustrates the relation between environmental irritation and constitutional resistance. You see there individuals I, II, and III opposed to environments 1, 2, and 3.

The resistance of individual I is minimal or insignificant, that of individual II is average, that of individual III is excessive. On the other hand, the irritations of environment 1 are minimal, those of 2 average, those of 3 excessive.

The Breakdown of Individual I Seems Unavoidable

We shall first consider individual I. His resistance to

INDIVIDUALS   **ENVIRONMENTS**

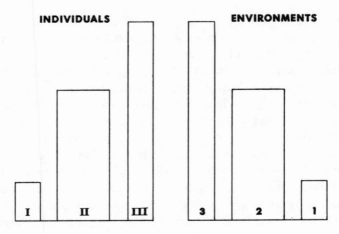

figure 1.

environmental stress is minimal. Even if placed in the placid atmosphere of environment 1 his break can hardly be prevented. His constitution is such that at some period of his existence he seems to be inescapably headed for a breakdown. If you happen to be the unfortunate relative of individual I, all your efforts to remove irritations from environment are likely to be futile. Experience gained from "shock" treatment indicates that if individual I responds favorably to therapy the response does not last. After a while he breaks again. With him both hospital treatment and after-care seem to be of little avail. I shall illustrate the situation by quoting a case history.

Case History of Individual I

John was 22 when his mind broke. Up to that time his development was that of the average boy. He enjoyed school and made the grades without difficulty. At play he was active although not a leader. In social contacts he contributed his share without being either conspicuous or retiring. He was employed as an electrician and did satisfactory work. His father died when John was a child and left the family in moderate financial circumstances. There was a close bond of affection between John, his mother, and an older sister. The home atmosphere was that of peace and comfort. One day, in his 22nd year, John suddenly arose during dinner, pointed to the wall, and exclaimed, "Why does that fellow stare at me?" Nobody but his mother and sister were in the room. They assured John that no man was present. But John insisted that the man on the wall cease staring at him. He was pale and trembled. A physician was called and the patient was put to sleep. In the morning he was in a daze and hallucinated about visions and voices. He was brought to the Psychopathic Hospital and admitted to the Psychiatric Institute. John went downhill rapidly and was soon reduced to a human hulk. His speech was an unintelligible babble and his behavior that of a baby, untidy and helpless. Today he is at the Chicago State Hospital where he leads a vegetative existence. Ever since his break seven years ago he has experienced few lucid moments.

Analysis of John's Case

The implications of John's case are simple. His environment was pleasant and congenial. Its irritations were reduced to a minimum. Obviously, environment was not the factor that broke John's mental health. Presumably John would have broken in any kind of environment.

If you glance at Figure 1 you will realize that John represents individual I who is placed in environment 1. We said that individual I is endowed with a minimum of resistance and that environment 1 offers a minimum of irritations. We may safely conclude that if John had lived in the more irritating atmosphere of environment 2, his health would have broken some time before his 22nd year—let me say, at the age of 18. Had he been exposed to environment 3, the break might have occurred even earlier, perhaps at 15 or 16.

What is it that you relatives of patients can learn from John's case? First: John's breakdown could hardly be prevented. Second: The fact that his mother provided him with the serenity of environment 1 was most likely the factor which rendered him capable of enjoying a life of fair adjustment up to his 22nd year. You see that even in the instance of individual I the conditions of home environment are responsible either for lengthening or shortening the period of normal adjustment.

Case History of Individual III

I shall now acquaint you briefly with the life history of an individual more or less the opposite of John. His name is Bob. His parents separated when the boy was four years old. The mother had no attachment for the child and boarded him out shortly after birth. After the mother died of a disease contracted in the course of a sordid life, the father remarried. Bob was now a stepchild and while not treated harshly missed the love of an affectionate mother. Due to a congenital shortsightedness his eyes bulged and he suffered agonies of inferiority on account of this defect. Boys teased him cruelly and girls shunned him because of his leering glance. In spite of this handicap he developed satisfactorily; he was described as "jovial, active, and full of life." In social gatherings he was "the life of the party." He was an excellent dancer. After leaving school, he secured a position in an insurance office and did good work. When, at 23, his mental health broke, he had already received three raises in salary. One day he joined his fellow employees in a gay party. He drank excessively and, returning home, molested a girl on the street. He was arrested and booked on a charge of disorderly conduct. The firm he worked with was notified by the police and the result was that Bob was discharged. When he came home that evening he did not speak, ate sparingly, and retired early. At night he awoke, ran to his father, and talked about "being advertised in the newspapers and over the radio." He claimed somebody took pictures of his eyes while he was in bed. In the morning he had alternate laughing and crying spells, and continually repeated the story that people talked about his defective eyes. He was taken to the Psychopathic Hospital and admitted to the Psychiatric Institute. Two weeks after arrival on the ward his anxiety was gone. He was quiet and no longer complained about being advertised and talked about. After another week he was ready to be discharged. He had been slated for "shock" treatment but had in the meantime recovered spontaneously.

Analysis of Bobs Case

Bob had the handicap of a lascivious mother who neglected him in early infancy and finally abandoned him. Brought up by strangers and subsequently by a tolerant but loveless stepmother he craved but missed affection. In addition, he had a marked visual defect, was the object of cruel taunting on the part of classmates, and was unsuccessful in his approach to girls. In spite of this, he developed an even temper, a pleasing disposition, social grace, and business efficiency. Moreover, when he broke, he recovered spontaneously before treatment could be administered.

In terms of Figure 1, Bob represents individual III, who is capable of asserting himself against the excessive irritations of environment 3. Had his relatives been able to provide for him a life in environment 1 or 2, we have good reason to doubt whether his mental health would have broken. Summing up, we may say: A congenial environment, relatively free from irritations, will help postpone the breakdown of individual I and will help prevent that of individual III.

Case History of Individual II

I shall now describe individual II. His name is George. His father was a successful architect and the mother an artist of local distinction. Due to her artistic preoccupation she entrusted the care of the baby to a nurse, later to a governess. Eating habits were poor from the start. Every bite required considerable coaxing. The boy could not be induced to eat unless stories were told or read to him. At kindergarten age he was tutored by a private teacher. At the age of six he entered a suburban public school. He showed fair ability but had difficulty getting along with his classmates. He was easily ruffled when unable to get his way. He complained currently of pains and aches, particularly when he met with difficulties of adjustment at school. After entering college, he again reacted with physical symptoms to the strain of examinations or other frustrations. On leaving college he secured a good position and held it in spite of the economic depression. At 24 he married. A substantial allowance from the father permitted him to live in relative comfort. But his marital life was punctuated by frequent friction. He was moody and sullen. His wife catered to his wishes but was unable to satisfy his whims. One day his father came to visit George and, on the occasion, presented him with a check. George tore the check to pieces and struck a violent blow at the father's face, exclaiming, "That's for causing all this trouble." He raved on for some time, demolished the furniture, broke a window, and had to be taken to a sanitarium. After a few months he was admitted to the Psychiatric Institute. There he received insulin shock treatment and was soon discharged as recovered.

Analysis of George's Case

That George was not endowed with an excessive degree of resistance is plain from his story. He was easily ruffled and frustrated. Due to his wilful temperament he fairly courted rebuffs. He fought the battle of life with moderate vigor, however, and can therefore not be called a individual with minimal resistance. In other words, George represented neither individual III nor individual I. His resistance was stronger than that of John but weaker than that of Bob. Expressed in terms of Figure 1, he represented individual II.

How was his environment? Was the amount of irritation it offered minimal, average, or excessive? He had a nurse, a governess, a private tutor; he enjoyed the advantages of wealth, passed high school, went to college, and obtained a good position. When he married and needed financial assistance, his father supplied it. Plainly his was a life of ease and comfort, and one might be inclined to identify his home setting with that of environment 1. However, an estimate of this kind would be based on an all too superficial concept of what environment means. And let me tell you: wealth and poverty are by no means the factors which determine whether an environment is pleasing or irritating. A child reared in the slums may grow up in harmony and another child surrounded by the splendor of a luxurious home may feel wretched and forlorn. Wealth and poverty touch on the material aspect of environment only. Its other aspect is ideational, and with regard to adjustment the ideational element is infinitely more important than its material counterpart. Measured by the standards of ideational elements, the setting in which George was reared must be considered as representing environment 2, perhaps even that of 3.

Material and Ideational Elements of Environment

I want you to grasp thoroughly the distinction between the material and ideational aspects of environment. You will then be better able to understand the basic differences between John's, Bob's, and George's developments. You will remember that I called John's environment congenial and harmonious. Yet, the family income was limited, just sufficient to supply the accommodations of a lower middle class home. Its congenial and harmonious atmosphere was certainly not the result of material comfort; it was rather due to such elements as mutual understanding, forbearance, and cooperation, in other words, to ideational factors. If you review Bob's history you will find a similar explanation for the disharmony from which he suffered. There was no material want in his home. His father was not a man of wealth but able to supply a reasonable measure of material comfort. What Bob suffered from was lack of affection on the part of the stepmother and from a sense of mortification in consequence of his visual defect. Affection and mortification must certainly be regarded as ideational elements. These examples will demonstrate clearly that it is the ideational factors which decide whether or not a given environment is conductive to adjustment. To express it in terms of Figure 1: Whether an environment offers a minimal, average, or excessive amount of irritations depends in the main on the ideational elements by which it is dominated. We have briefly traced the effect of these ideational influences in John's and Bob's environments 1 and 3. It will be the object of our next lecture to study the same ideational elements in environment 2, which seems to be that of George. Since it is the ideational factors mainly which determine the peacefulness or disharmony of an environment, you may safely conclude that the after-care which you are to provide for the returned patient can only be secured if you somehow learn (1) to recognize, (2) to control ideational influences.

The reader will notice that the lectures place the emphasis on the home situation, with forceful stress on environment as ideational influence. In subsequent lectures, this ideational factor will be plainly designated as the excessive concerns, anxieties and aggressions of parental, fraternal and uxorial tempers. Control of temper and training of will are the main themes of the subsequent lectures.

LECTURE 2

HOME ADJUSTMENT AND AFTER-CARE

We shall continue the discussion of George's case. You remember that George represented individual II who was placed in environment 2. You also remember that individual II was described as being endowed with *average* resistance, and environment 2 as offering the *average* amount of irritations. If this be so we are reasonably certain that in discussing George we are discussing the *average recovered* patient. When George broke down he raved, struck his father, demolished the furniture and smashed a window. Behavior of this kind is plainly maladjusted, uncontrolled and unbalanced. From this you may infer that without a mental breakdown, average behavior is ordinarily adjusted, controlled and balanced. It will be our task now to discuss the meaning of the terms adjustment, control and balance.

The Meaning of an Act Must Be Adjusted to That of the Corresponding Event

Briefly, what is adjusted or maladjusted is the *act of behavior;* what is controlled or uncontrolled are *impulses,* what is balanced or unbalanced are the major functions of mentality, i.e., *emotion and intellect.* When George struck his father "without sane reason," the act of striking (not of behavior) was maladjusted, his impulse to strike was uncontrolled, and emotion or intellect were thrown out of their customary balance.

You recall the sequence of events on the occasion of George's breakdown. His father presented him with a check. George tore it up, struck the blow and exclaimed, "That's for causing all this trouble." At that moment, the

25

father offering the check was the main factor in George's environment, and the raving, the blow, and the wild exclamations were the acts of behavior with which he responded. The meaning of the environmental event was that of a friendly approach, and the meaning of George's act of behavior was that of a hostile reaction. The two meanings contradicted one another and were not mutually adjusted. Behavior was maladjusted.

You will find in Figure 2 (page 27) an illustration of the relationship between events of environment and acts of behavior. The circle in the center of the figure represents the individual (Ind.). To the left of the circle are listed the varieties of events which act on the individual. They are either hostile (1), or neutral (2), or friendly (3). Examples of hostile events are: acts of violence, threats, irritating remarks, severe criticism, refusal of requests. Neutral events are: the church bell striking twelve, a street car stopping at the corner, a stranger asking the time. Friendly events: a letter announcing promotion, a child being born, a daughter getting married.

To the right of the circle you notice acts of behavior proceeding from or being produced by the individual. They are either hostile (I), or neutral (II), or friendly (III). The terms are self-explanatory. You will now understand that if the conduct of an individual is to be adjusted his acts of behavior must have the same meanings (hostile, neutral, friendly) as the corresponding events of environment. In other words, if an individual meets with event 1 he ought to respond with act I; to event 2, the adjusted reaction is act II; to event 3, act III. George's father bringing a check represented event 3 (friendly). George, striking out, responded with act I (hostile). The friendly meaning of the environmental event 3 clashed with and contradicted the hostile meaning of act I, and George's conduct became maladjusted.

There are occasions when a hostile event (1) may be met with a friendly act (III) and behavior may remain normal,

EVENTS   ACTS OF BEHAVIOR

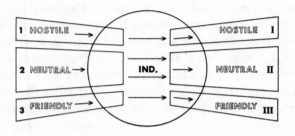

figure 2

nevertheless. For instance, a mother may be insulted by her son and reciprocate with loving kindness. But this is special maternal behavior, not *average* reaction.

Events Are Experienced as Irritating, Stimulating or Neutral

Figure 3, below, leads us one step further in the analysis of George's behavior. You see there the individual (circle), the events to the left (1, 2, 3), and the acts of behavior to

EVENTS   ACTS OF BEHAVIOR

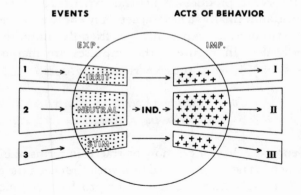

figure 3

the right (I, II, III). An event is a mere happening and may or may not be noticed by the individual. But once it is noticed it is *experienced*. The experience (Exp. in Figure 3) is either emotional or intellectual, but usually a combination of both. For instance, a gun pointed at me is an event. If I notice it I first know that I am in danger (intellectual experience), second, I have the emotion of fear (emotional experience). Similarly, if I receive a gift I first know that something was sent me by somebody (intellectual experience), second, I feel the emotion of joy (emotional experience). Experience 1 is the result of a hostile event and is irritating or provoking; experience 3, being the result of a friendly event, is stimulating; and experience 2, produced by a neutral event, is neither irritating nor stimulating. It is neutral.

An irritating experience may give rise to a fighting or hostile impulse. (Imp. in Figure 3) The hostile impulse thereupon releases a hostile act of behavior. Figure 3 shows that each experienced event produced its corresponding impulse which then releases the corresponding act of behavior. We can now sum up: in adjusted behavior a hostile event produces an irritating experience; it then gives rise to a hostile impulse and releases a hostile act. A neutral event produces a neutral experience, a neutral impulse and, finally, a neutral act. A friendly event results in a stimulating experience, a friendly impulse and friendly act. In Figure 3 the impulses are marked by crosses (+   +   +), the experiences by dots (: : : :).

Correct Acting Depends on Correct Experiencing of Events

George's behavior can now be traced in terms of Figure 3. When his father presented him with the check the event had a friendly meaning and ought to have produced a stimulating experience. Instead, it gave rise to an irritating experience. The irritation aroused a hostile impulse and was followed by a hostile act. We conclude that George's hostile act was the result of a faulty experience and suspect that correct and adjusted acting depends on correct experiencing of events.

The Relatives' Actions May Be Irritating Events

There is a fateful lesson in this for you relatives of former patients. Your mode of acting, your manner of statement, your attitudes, moods and dispositions are the principal events of environment, to which the former patient reacted prior to his breakdown and to which he reacts now that he is discharged. Whatever you do or say, whatever you express in plain acts or words, or in the more subtle manifestations of harsh intonations, ironical smiles, forbidding frowns, contemptuous shrugs and unsympathetic gestures are events which produce experiences and impulses in the central nervous system of your returned son, brother or husband. This is the reason why you must learn to regulate your conduct in such a manner that the environmental events which you represent do not produce too many irritating experiences. Your task is all the more difficult because the discharged patient is usually *recovering and not yet fully recovered*. A recovering patient is likely to experience as irritating many events which, to the ordinary individual, are neutral and innocuous.

A Diseased Brain Misjudged Environmental Events

When George struck out at his father his brain was diseased. One of the main functions of the brain is to judge the meaning of environmental events. A diseased brain is likely to misjudge events and may, for instance, perceive friendly motives as hostile intentions. It will be necessary for you to know something about how a healthy brain judges environmental events. Figure 4 (page 30) gives a graphic account of the processes involved. You see there

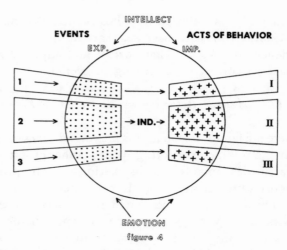

figure 4

exactly the same arrangement of events, experiences, impulses and actions as in Figure 3. However, at the top of the figure you read the words "intellect," and at the bottom "emotion." The arrows which proceed from the top and bottom words indicate that both experiences (Exp.) and impulses (Imp.) are subject to emotional and intellectual judgment.

Balance Between Emotional and Intellectual Judgment

I shall ask you to recall an occasion when a barking dog suddenly darted out of a hallway and jumped at you while you walked leisurely along the sidewalk. You had the experience of a startle and felt scared. Then you looked about and realized, i.e., judged that the barking dog was nothing to be afraid of. Presently the fear was gone and calm returned. In this instance the environmental event of the leaping dog was first experienced as danger by your emotional judgment but subsequently conceived as harmless (neutral) by your intellectual judgment. Intellect corrected the error produced by emotion. Had intellect not been called into action the emotion of fear would have precipitated a rash impulse, and you might have kicked the dog or run away from him. In that event, emotion would have held sway over your action without being properly checked or counterbalanced by intellect. Without proper balance between intellect and emotion, your mind would have been *unbalanced*—for a brief moment.

George's Emotions Checkmated His Intellect

Whenever an individual is overpowered by emotion he is thrown out of balance. Ecstasy, enthusiasm, infatuation, fear, rage, jealousy, horror and consternation are familiar examples. If the brain is intact emotional upheavals of this kind are easily brought under control again and the balance restored. George's brain was diseased and his unbalanced manner of experiencing events continued unabated for weeks. When he was admitted to the Psychiatric Institute he was no longer acutely disturbed. He answered questions correctly, cooperated with ward routine, slept and ate well. However, he had ideas which defied sane argument. Over and again he repeated, "I am going to die. They are going to burn me this afternoon." In the evening he was told, "George, you said they were going to burn you this afternoon, but they didn't. Don't you think you were wrong?" His reply was, "Oh, they just put it off another day. But tomorrow they are going to kill me." Daily, for weeks, he predicted his death for the afternoon and daily, in the evening, the absurdity of his prediction was demonstrated to him. His stock reply was, "But tomorrow they are going to kill me." Emotion had checkmated intellect, and argument was wasted. His mind was unbalanced.

Emotional-Intellectual Imbalance Leads to Loss of Control of Impulses

Thus far we have discussed George's behavior from the viewpoint of adjustment (of acts to events) and balance (between emotion and intellect). It remains to consider the third element of behavior: control (of impulses). When George conceived of his father as a hostile influence his emotional-intellectual balance was upset and he instantly released a hostile impulse (to strike a blow). In ordinary life people lose their balance frequently under stress of emotion but they do not necessarily release violent impulses. Instead, they check the impulses and keep them under control. Indeed, with normally responsive persons, hardly a day ever passes but they become incensed at some offense or misdemeanor, actually or supposedly committed by a colleague, employee, son, pupil. Violent impulses of wrath, indignation, and resentment are then aroused, ready to be released. But intellect intercedes and cautions against hasty reactions. The impulses are restrained and refused expression. When George, in the early stage of his breakdown, lost his balance he also lost control of impulses. Henceforth, and for some time, his acts were maladjusted, his experiences unbalanced and his impulses uncontrolled.

His Wife's Apprehension Became a Source of Irritation After George's Recovery

After several weeks of insulin treatment, George recovered sufficiently to be credited by the staff with balanced experiences, control of impulses and adjustment of acting. He was pronounced recovered and returned to his family. His wife was overjoyed and eager to cater to his welfare. Unfortunately, her eagerness was overdone. She incessantly asked him how he felt and whether he was tired. She cautioned him to take it easy when he took a walk, and urged him not to strain his eyes when he prepared to read the paper. At meals she showed alarm that his water might be too cold, his soup too hot, and the vegetable not sufficiently digestible for his weak stomach. She supervised his moves, regulated his activities, decreed how long he had to rest on the couch, at what hour he was to retire. When he desired to visit a friend she interposed her veto on the grounds that he must "take it easy." The result was that George felt watched, under scrutiny and suspicion. The physicians had declared him recovered but his wife still treated him as a patient. He protested against the interference but the wife stood her ground and insisted on compliance. After a while he rebelled against her meddling and disregarded her dictates. She remonstrated with him; she pleaded, begged and warned but without success. Finally she went into hysterics, invoked the specter of relapse, and disclaimed responsibility should he have to be returned to the hospital. "If you break down again it will all be your own fault," she exclaimed with agonizing frequency. George had recovered but was now exposed to a constant stream of irritating domestic events which threatened again to disturb his balance, to unleash his impulses and to maladjust his acts of behavior. His wife's uncalled for apprehensiveness was the source of these irritating events.

The Patient's Appeal to the Physicians for Help

Like so many patients who recovered after successful treatment, George was attached to the hospital and genuinely appreciative of what the physicians had done for him. Oppressed by his wife's oversolicitude he appealed to them for help and advice. Soon other patients came with their tales of domestic friction. We were suddenly confronted with the fact that the patient, after being cured of his "abnormal" behavior, must be protected from the "normal" misbehavior of his relatives. The irritable dispositions and undisciplined tempers of those at home were bound to act as "hostile events" and likely to release "hostile impulses." The patient was again in danger of becoming "unbalanced," unless the relatives learned how to govern their tempers and idiosyncrasies. As a result you were invited to attend these conferences. I hope I shall be able, in the next series of lectures, to impress on you the importance of checking your tempers and softening your dispositions in order to provide a reasonable quality of aftercare for the returned patient.

———————

Like most lectures presented in this book the one reproduced in the present chapter was given in four separate installments covering four successive biweekly Sunday meetings. In each of them the importance of domestic temper was stressed with increasing force. The passage on page 29 beginning with, "There is a fateful lesson in this for you relatives . . . " represents the core of the writer's views on domestic discord in its relation to aftercare. Briefly stated it postulates that the attitudes, moods and dispositions of the relatives are the principal events of environment to which the returned patient has to adjust. Environment is here described as a dynamic force liable to change and correction on the part of those persons who are the "principal events" in the patient's surroundings. The view presents nothing original but the sharp emphasis placed on it is missing in contemporary psychiatric literature. The group psychotherapist will be at a disadvantage if he neglects to accept the emphasis. If he adopts it he will make the relatives share the responsibility for future relapses. In raising the issue of domestic temper, Recovery, Inc. has aroused the conscience of many relatives who heretofore had shirked their part of the responsibility. That the success is not complete, that many relatives are little touched by Recovery's teaching, goes without saying. The record is nevertheless impressive. Both our own observations and the voluntary admissions of parents and spouses give eloquent testimony to the effectiveness of our insistence on temper control.

Another emphasis, merely foreshadowed in the present lecture but elaborately treated in subsequent discourses, is that on average reactions and adjustment to average events. This point will be adverted to currently in the majority of the lectures.

Summing up: The main subject matter discussed in Recovery, Inc. meetings is temper as evidenced in the average reaction of the average individual when confronted with the average trivialities of everyday life.

LECTURE 3

THE "CONDITIONAL" STANDARD
OF BEHAVIOR

Our discussion ought to have made it clear to you that the most important factor in the regulation of behavior is the proper emotional-intellectual balance. We shall now turn to a detailed analysis of this balance.

Emotions Are a Team, Managed by Intellect

Emotion and intellect are frequently called a team. You know a team of horses, a baseball team, a team of workingmen. Teams of this kind perform work under the direction of a leader. The driver, the captain and foreman supply the leadership.

In a team the leader balances the action of the teammates. In a baseball group, for instance, the manager determines which men are to pitch, which to act as infielders, which as outfielders. In a given club there may be thirty players. If an act of baseball behavior (league game) is to be released the manager decides which players to choose and which to reject. A wrong choice may result in an unbalanced team. Several of the team members may be eager to do the pitching. It is the manager's task to assign the function to the most suitable man. Note that the players are many but there must be one manager only.

Emotions function as a team with intellect as their manager. There are many emotions but there should be one intellect only. This means that intellect must not be *divided* by several conflicting thoughts but must be *determined* by one leading idea. Intellect, as the team manager, determines which member of the emotional team should, at a given moment, be accorded the privilege to release a corresponding act of behavior, and which are to be restrained. If intellect displays managing ability the emotional team will be well balanced.

Intellect Guides Emotional Team by Means of Standard of Behavior

To conduct a game properly the manager must rely on a set of rules. Otherwise the activities of the team members may become chaotic due to the changing whims of the manager. The set of rules by means of which intellect guides the team of emotions is called *standard of behavior*.

The main standards of behavior are (1) legal, (2) moral, (3) ethical, (4) esthetic, (5) conditional. The term "conditional" requires explanation. It refers to behavior which while ordinarily not regulated by standards may, "under certain conditions," become subject to regulation. If a man wishes to eat a sandwich there is no rule of conduct that standardizes the act. Under ordinary circumstances, he may consume it or leave it untouched. He may swallow it quickly or leisurely. He may choose thick or thin slices and dress them with ham, cheese, beef, and what not. Under "certain conditions," however, the act or manner of eating the sandwich may be an offense against the spirit of the just prevailing situation. You would certainly rate it a serious breach of etiquette should I now, while lecturing to you, produce a sandwich and eat it. The sandwich is tabu "under the conditions" of this lecture. I shall briefly quote similar examples. When at home I am permitted to dress or undress as I choose. But "conditions" change when I leave the home. Then I *must* be dressed. Similarly, at home I may smoke, at a concert I must not. At home I may whistle, sing, hum and yawn but when interviewed by my prospective employer the whistling, singing, humming and yawning would inevitably be interpreted as improper conduct.

*The Average Person Respects Legal, Moral
and Ethical Standards*

I mentioned five standards. This list is by no means exhaustive. The standards of logic and grammar were omitted as relatively unimportant from the viewpoint of adjustment. Strange as it may seem, the conditional standard is perhaps generally, but certainly for the relatives of former patients of far greater adjustive importance than the legal, moral, ethical and esthetic standards. You will readily see why. Our main interest is focused on your behavior toward the patient when he returns home. Now there is no doubt that you, your wife, son and daughter will not offend against the legal, moral and ethical standards. We can take it for granted that the relatives of our patients are not given to burglary, thievery, treachery and trickery. Should it ever happen that a parent of one of our patients turns out to be legally or ethically irresponsible the case would be exceptional, not *average*. And you remember that our discussion is concerned with *average behavior* only. In the sphere of average behavior illegal conduct has hardly any place. Neither has frankly immoral or unethical practice.

I know that in a number of homes to which our patients return there is little regard for the so-called esthetic standard. From the reports of our social workers and from personal experience I know that the environment to which the recovered patient is sent is not always a model of cleanliness. In some of the homes there is good evidence of occasional spitting and tobacco chewing, and I have been told that in a number of our families slang and profanity are not completely banned. Now, don't think for a moment that I approve of untidiness, spitting and profanity. But no matter how intensely I dislike these esthetically reprehensible habits I should be guilty of an untruth should I rate them too high in the scheme of *average adjustment*.

Practical Intellect Decided Which Acts Are
Called-for or Uncalled-for

Our main interest is then centered on the conditional standard. The remarkable thing about this standard is that what it regulates are acts which seem devoid of social importance. I quoted the act of eating a sandwich, of dressing and undressing, of smoking, whistling, humming, singing and yawning. I could have added as long a tabulation of trivial acts as would cover the endless range of everyday life. What could be more trivial than the desire to take off one's shoes or to inspect one's shirt or to scratch one's head. At certain times, in certain places and under certain conditions, acts of this kind are innocent and harmless; but at other times, in other places and under other conditions, they constitute a serious offense against etiquette. They are innocent and harmless when performed in the privacy of the home but inexcusable at a public gathering, in church, at a concert, during an interview. There they lose their innocence and become irritating and offensive. To sum up: The conditional standard demands that acts of behavior which are innocuous from the legal, moral, ethical and esthetic viewpoint be so adjusted to the *requirements of time, place and circumstances* that they are *timely, in their proper place and suited to the circumstances* of the situation. Otherwise they are *untimely, out of place and unsuited to the circumstances*. The acts which are timely, in their proper place and suited to the circumstances are said to be *called-for* by the circumstances of the situation. The others are *uncalled-for*. We can now state our final formulation: The conditional standard determines which acts of behavior are called-for or uncalled-for by the requirements of time, place and circumstances of a given situation. Whether an act of behavior is called-for or uncalled-for is decided by practical judgment or practical intellect.

*Adjustment to Great Upheavals Is Easier Than to
Everyday Irritations*

Current psychologies stress the momentous events in
life. Their examples and illustrations are usually taken
from the field of emergencies, calamities, grave errors,
fatal omissions, war, imprisonment, bankruptcy. These
momentous events are rare exceptions in the lifetime of an
individual. How often does the *average person* suffer
bankruptcy? How often does he go to prison? How often is
he the victim of calamitous emergencies or fatal errors?
The answer is clear: Momentous events are interesting
from the viewpoint of intellectual curiosity but relatively
unimportant in the scheme of average adjustment.

The average individual adjusts with comparative ease to
the great upheavals of life. During the world war men
suffered agonies of hunger, fatigue and pain; mothers lost
their sons, wives their husbands, children their fathers.
After a relatively short time the wounds were healed and
readjustment effected. The economic depression of 1929
taught a similar lesson. Fortunes were lost and existences
destroyed overnight. If the victim was an average
individual he adjusted to the new situation within a short
period.

What taxes the adjustive capacity of the average
individual are the more or less continuous, repetitious and
habitual irritations of common everyday life. Calamities
and disasters are hardly ever habitual; small irritations
frequently are. I mentioned that in the sphere of average
life there is no habitual bankruptcy, no habitual
imprisonment or war service. But there are habitual
quibblings between husband and wife; there are habitual
tauntings, criticisms, suspicions, jealousies, incrimina-
tions and rancors. If you relatives of our patients indulge
habitually in any one of these features you create a home
atmosphere to which the returned patient will hardly be
able to adjust his *recovering* sensibilities. If you wish to

avoid the dire consequences of your sarcastic, critical, suspicious, jealous, incriminatory or rancorous temper you will have to learn to master the conditional standard.

Edna's Behavior Was of Poor Average Quality

We shall return to our case discussion. It will be plain to you that George's wife—we shall call her Edna—was an average woman. There are three main varieties of averageness. A person may be *good average, plain average and poor average.* This threefold division applies to every human trait. Take the average physician, lawyer or merchant. In points of efficiency, industry, ambition, loyalty, civic mindedness, sympathy, they all may be good, plain or poor average. Let me tell you that if a patient is returned to your home you must somehow endeavor to develop a type of behavior that is good or plain average. It must not be poor average. Edna's behavior fell into the category of poor average.

What precisely was it that made Edna's behavior so poor in average quality? She asked George frequently how he felt and whether he was tired. She voiced fears that his food was too hot or too cold. She cautioned him to take it easy and to refrain from exerting himself. This was apparently the expression of concern, interest and sympathy. If anything, it ought to represent good average reaction. Why, then, did I say that Edna's behavior must be rated as of poor average quality?

Acts Have Direct Expressions and Indirect Implications

An act of behavior consists of (1) *a direct expression,* (2) *an indirect implication.* Suppose you see a man suddenly jumping to his feet; he gesticulates with fury, his face flushed, his cheeks tense, the eyes flashing and the tone of voice harsh and strident. Finally, he strikes another man in the face, yelling, "I'll teach you how to behave in the presence of a lady."

What you saw and heard could be *observed* directly by your eyes and ears. Hence, the term *direct expression*. The act which you witnessed offered many expressions. They were verbal (the spoken sentence), motor (the striking arm), vocal (the harsh tone of voice). There were other directly observable expressions: the flashing of the eyes, the flush of the face, the tenseness of the cheeks, the gesticulating of the arms prior to striking the blow. One might add: the widening of the nostrils, the heavy breathing, perhaps also the gnashing of teeth. But I shall not burden you with an avalanche of details. What I want you to know is that an act of behavior finds its direct expression mainly in (1) verbal, (2) motor, (3) vocal reactions, (4) in gestures, (5) in facial features.

Jealous Act Violates Conditional Standard

From what you observed directly you conclude that one man was in rage after another insulted a lady. You may be inclined to add that the man who struck the blow was not only in rage but that his rage was justified because it was intended to avenge an insult to a defenseless woman. At this point you credit both the striking and the struck man with intentions and motives. The one man intended to insult a woman, and the other intended to avenge her. It will not be difficult for you to realize that motives and intentions cannot be observed directly; they must be inferred or implied indirectly from the observed expressions of an act. We conclude that the expressions of an act of behavior can be observed directly by the senses. Its implications (motives) can be only inferred indirectly by judgment.

After the tumult dies down you inquire about the particulars of the scene and learn that the man who received the blow did nothing more than address an innocent pleasantry to the lady in question. Nobody in the group conceived of this remark as offensive or insulting. You further hear that the man who flew into a rage is the jealous suitor of the lady, who resents attentions paid her by others. You now conclude that the act of striking was not justified. Remembering the terms which I used a short while ago you will argue that violence might have been called for *under conditions* of an actual insult to a lady but was uncalled for *under conditions* of sheer jealousy. When the provoked suitor gave direct expression to his jealous temper he violated the *conditional* standard of average behavior.

Verbal and Motor Expressions of Hostility Are Uncivilized

Jealousy is an emotion with hostile intentions. You recall my statement that acts of behavior can be given direct expression in (1) words, (2) motor reactions, (3) vocal intonations, (4) gestures, (5) facial features. It is an established rule of the conditional standard that, in the average civilized group, hostile intentions must not be given direct expression in words or in motor reactions. In order to be credited with the status of average civility a man must not utter threats or other words of violent intention and must not strike blows or execute similar crude acts. Violent gestures are generally also frowned upon by the conditional standard but are not as severely condemned as verbal and motor hostility. Hostility expressed in mere vocal intonation and in facial expression is by no means approved by the conditional standard but is not branded as uncivilized.

Uncivilized verbal and motor behavior is not called for by average circumstances. Under exceptional conditions it is sometimes sanctioned, for instance, when a lady is insulted. Under ordinary conditions, uncivilized conduct is not even of poor average quality; it is simply not average.

Since the subject of our discussion is precisely that of average reaction we are not interested in the topic of motor or verbal violence. We take it for granted that our patients will not be subject to raw abuse, beatings and wild threats on the part of their relatives when they return home from the hospital

Edna's Behavior Was Not Uncivilized

Edna, George's wife, was obviously not uncivilized. She was not given to verbal or motor brutality. Her behavior was still within the range of the average. But throughout this discussion I considered her poor average. What is the reason for this low rating?

We said that Edna gave George constant advice and instruction. It will be important for you relatives to realize that even the most innocent performance becomes tiring and annoying if it is repeated too frequently. Nothing is more innocent than for a mother to ask her son, "How are you?" But if this innocent question is repeated on twenty successive occasions, at ten wrong times, in ten wrong places the question is still innocent but—annoying. The implication is unavoidable that the mother thinks the son is still in need of maternal supervision. If that son has just passed through a mental ailment the implication has a particularly irritating effect. The son is now forcefully reminded—rightly or wrongly—that the mother distrusts the permanency or effectiveness of his recovery.

Edna did not confine herself to asking innocent questions. She incessantly directed George what to do and what to avoid. All George had to do was to place the spoon on the napkin in order to rearrange his seat when his wife, in a flash of unmistakable anger, exclaimed, "But, dear, how often must I tell you not to let your soup get cold?" On numerous occasions she passed remarks like, "Why do you make it so difficult for me? Didn't I suffer enough when you were sick? Do you want me to go through all this again? If you don't mind your own health can't you at least have some consideration for me and the children?" You remember I stated that, "Finally she went into hysterics, invoked the specter of relapse and disclaimed responsibility should he have to be returned to the hospital. 'If you break down again it will all be your fault,' she exclaimed with agonizing frequency." (See page 33)

Edna Was Civilized But Not Cultured

If you keep in mind the five types of expressions I spoke about you will understand that Edna avoided rude words and brusque acts. Her verbal and motor expressions were not uncivilized. But her voice trembled with harsh undertones, her gestures betrayed annoyance and impatience, and her features were set and resentful. If her criticisms were actuated by feelings of concern and wifely apprehension why did she express harshness, impatience and set determination in voice, gestures and features? If her motor and verbal behavior meant kind consideration why did voice, gestures, and features indicate antagonism and bellicosity?

In a subsequent lecture I shall dwell at length on the meaning of this contradictory type of behavior. For the present, I content myself with stating that Edna gave vent to her rancor in tones, gestures and features but suppressed it in words and acts. Mark that no matter how carefully you choose your words and how skillfully you control your acts your returned son, brother and husband will inevitably take offense if your verbal and motor sweetness is plainly contradicted by the sournesss and roughness of your voice, gestures and features.

Edna was obviously of a belligerent disposition. She tended to be domineering and dictatorial. When she controlled her domineering tendencies in her verbal and motor behavior she was civilized, i.e., average. But when she failed to control it in intonation, features and gestures she was uncultured, i.e., poor average. I add that if I speak of culture I do not merely refer to the culture of the intellect but in a far greater measure to that of emotions. Edna was a college graduate, fairly well grounded in art and literature; she attended courses and lectures and displayed good taste in the choice of her reading. Her intellect was trained but undisciplined; her emotions were a wild, chaotic team without proper leadership.

The concept of the "conditional" as contrasted with the legal, moral, ethical and esthetic standards is fundamental to the system of instruction given by the author. It is contrary to the thesis silently maintained or vocally expressed by most persons that a man has done his duty if he is law-abiding, loyal to family, country and friends, honest in business deals, and jealous of proprieties in general. This doctrine of "doing one's duty" to the recognized standards leaves out of consideration the trivialities of everyday life. After a man has curbed his illegal, immoral, unethical and unesthetic inclinations he is permitted to give free rein to those dispositions which are not included in the regulations of the official and relatively "unconditional" standards. In the Recovery, Inc. system of teaching the proportions are reversed. The relatives are told over and again that what is most in need of strict observance is the "conditional" standard of unofficial, domestic, trivial everyday behavior. The officially regulated spheres of civic life, social commerce, business enterprise and other "important and significant" fields of existence need correspondingly less watching because with the average person it has become "second nature" to pay homage to the rules governing this part of his conduct.

LECTURE 4

THE MAJOR MOTIVES OF BEHAVIOR

Edna's behavior was civilized but not cultured. As such we characterized it as of poor average quality and concluded that for behavior to be plain or good average it must be cultured and not *merely* civilized.

Service and Domination Are the Principal Motives

Behavior, if it is not reflex, is guided by intentions or motives. There are two main varieties of motives: service and domination. Love, friendship, admiration, neighborliness, civic-mindedness, patriotism, honesty in business dealings, ethical conduct in professional affairs, loyalty to men and causes, plain courtesy and civility, are all prompted by the motive of service. Hatred, enmity, contempt, dissension, rascality, hypocrisy, jealousy, envy, discourtesy and incivility are the product of the motive of domination.

In average life, neither the motive of service nor that of domination exist in their pure state. A person inspired by the spirit of service exclusively would be a saint; one inspired by the sole urge for domination would be a monster. Neither fits into the scheme of average life. Both are exceptional and extreme in their motivations.

The average person is activated by both major motives and tends both to serve and to dominate. This existence, side by side, of two mutually contradictory motives cannot be overemphasized if the problems of the recovered patient are to be discussed properly. When your son or daughter, husband or wife is returned to you, you will, at the same time, try to serve and to dominate them. You would not be human if you did not do so.

47

The Two Major Motives Require a Healthy Balance

How can two opposite trends of behavior be enacted coincidently? The answer is: by means of a *healthy balance*. A healthy balance of the two major motives makes for healthy group life. Group life turns into endless strife if those sharing it insist on domination exclusively. It is monotonous, colorless, and "lifeless" if nothing but service prevails.

You know the game called "tug of war." One set of people tug at the one end of a rope, another at the other end. If the pulling strength of the two groups is *equally balanced* there will be no action. On the other hand, if the distribution of forces is *too unequally balanced*, there will be no contest. One of the groups will have a "walkaway." A healthy contest will ensue only if the pull of the one team *just over-balances* that of the other. This example will show you what is meant by a healthy balance. A balance is healthy if the opposing forces are neither equally nor too unequally matched. In the field of motives, a healthy balance is maintained if service over balances domination without overwhelming or eliminating it.

Rude Behavior Is More Common at Home Than on the Outside

It is a popular belief contrary to actual experience that the spirit of service is generously displayed in the home sphere and that the spirit of domination increases the more the sphere of action includes strangers. According to this theory, relatives are generally approached in the spirit of service, strangers in that of domination. If this were so, irritation and annoyance would be rare at home and abundantly experienced in the company of strangers. However, if you consult your own past record you will realize that the bulk of your irritations stem from your close relatives and friends, that a smaller but considerable portion of annoyance can be traced back to your coworkers and card game partners, and that the strangers whom you meet in the department store or in the street car are seldom a source of irritation or provocation. In other words, the average individual tries his best to be friendly and courteous with the stranger but loses his temper frequently with those familiar to him and is likely to be rude and impatient with his intimates. The reason for this discriminating behavior is clear; you risk nothing or little if you are harsh and brusque with your son, father, or mother. They are helpless in the face of your rudeness. What disciplinary measure can a mother resort to if her son is intractable? She cannot very well eject him and deny him his share of family life. Her love renders her a victim of the son's incivility. Let the same son display his rudeness in the presence of strangers, and he will not be permitted to victimize any of them. They will not hesitate to pay him back in kind.

You all know of the husband who frequently, and without compunction, is late for dinner at home and practically always ahead of time when expected at the house of a friend or stranger. Should it happen that, through some unforeseen circumstance, he is prevented from being punctual for the outside engagement, he is certain to telephone and to offer profuse apologies. No apology is even thought of if the delay merely concerns the dinner arrangement at home. In this instance, the punctuality and the apology to the hostess are the expression of a spirit of service and the lack of courtesy displayed to the wife an exhibit of domination.

The Problem Adult Displays "Devil-at-Home-Angel-Abroad" Attitude

In this husband's pattern of behavior, domination has a "walkaway" at home and service abroad. There is no healthy balance between the two sets of motives. The two forces are altogether too unequally distributed over the divergent spheres of life. Behavior of this kind goes by the name of the "devil-at-home-angel-abroad" attitude. It is a common pattern among children, and a child praticing it to excess may be called a "problem child." It has struck me that I am frequently told of problem children but seldom of problem husbands and wives, mothers and fathers. True enough, the average wife and husband, mother and father, do not in the fashion of problem children throw tantrums or break china. However, if problem behavior at least in one of its manifestations is characterized by domination at home and service abroad, the terms "problem husband," "problem wife," "problem father," and "problem mother" ought to have equal rank with the term "problem child." They ought to be considered its most common adult equivalent.

Edna was a problem wife, i.e., a problem adult. In her contacts with outsiders she was a model of gentleness and civility. She was known as a charming hostess and delightful guest. She went out of her way to please friends and acquaintances and was careful not to be overbearing or imposing. Her smile was winning and her manner engaging. In contrast to this graceful conduct in social settings her behavior at home was marked by impatience and irritability. True, she was not violent, vituperative or profane. But her charming ways simply evaporated the moment she crossed the threshold of her home. On the outside she was cultured and refined, at home *merely* civilized and—not exactly coarse.

I do not wish to be too critical but cannot help stating it as my opinion that too many of you relatives of patients are problem adults. Too many of you, although well behaved in social contacts, tend to display a relentless trend toward domination when dealing with members of your own family. If this is true the recovered patient, on returning home, will face an atmosphere of harshness and impatience that is likely to break again his restored health. If this calamity is to be avoided, those of you who conduct yourselves as problem adults will have to learn how to acquire the manners and attitudes of normally balanced individuals.

Temperaments and Dispositions Can Be Changed Through Determination and Insight

Both domination and service are based on what is called *disposition,* or *temperament.* The spirit of domination gives rise to or stems from the competitive or domineering temperament, that of service has a similar relation to the cooperative or submissive temperament. The implication is that if the relative of a patient is advised to mend his domineering ways he is asked to change a disposition or a temperament. Is this possible? The answer is: it has been done frequently, hence, it can be done. Indeed, if tempers and dispositions could not be changed what would be the rationale of trying to influence men by means of religious, educational and artistic endeavors?

There is much talk these days about adult education. As a psychiatrist I claim practical experience in this field. For many years I made an effort to re-educate adult persons and secured a measure of success. But I never obtained satisfactory results unless I was able to give the patient *insight* into his failings. It is an axiom of psychotherapy that a set of dynamic habits (dispositions or temperaments) cannot be changed unless (1) the patient is determined to effect a change, (2) the psychiatrist is able to make the patient see his handicap. By making the patient realize the nature of his shortcomings the psychiatrist gives him insight into them.

Edna had no insight into her shortcomings. She was simply not aware of their existence. She was convinced that her actions were animated by the very noblest intentions and that her conduct was dictated solely by the sense of responsibility and the spirit of devotion. In her mind there was no question that she was right and her husband wrong. This assurance of oneself being right and the other person wrong is the essential basis of what I described as the domestic attitude of the problem adult. It is the rock on which most unsuccessful marital relations are currently wrecked.

Temperaments Are Concealed in Words and Acts and Revealed in Tones, Gestures and Features

It is a comparatively rare occurrence among relatives or friends of average breeding that one person takes offense at the words or acts of the other. However, it is a common experience that relatives and friends hurt and irritate one another by means of tone, gesture and feature. Every civilized person has learned to control words and motor acts. Even if his temperament is competitive and domineering he will take care not to give it verbal and motor expression. The calamity is that unless a person is a supreme actor he has little practice in the control of tones, gestures and features. It may be stated as a fact that if a person is possessed of a domineering temper he will *conceal* it in words and acts but *reveal* it in tone, gesture and feature.

Like so many "temperamental" persons, Edna was too impetuous to be sufficiently on guard in choosing her words. A good deal of her domineering disposition was, therefore, revealed even in her address. You remember I told you that in her eagerness to superintend George's daily life she passed on numerous occasions remarks like, "Why do you make it so difficult for me? Didn't I suffer enough when you were sick? Do you want me to go through all this again? If you don't mind your own health, can't you at least have some consideration for me and the children?" (See page 44) These questions contained no verbal or motor indication of rudeness or hostility. Edna did not swear or yell. On the face of it, her harangue was in the form of a plea or request and devoid of threats or invective. However, when she asked, "Why do you *make* it so difficult for me?" the implication was that George contrived to *make* difficulties for her. When she continued, "Do you *want* me to go through all this again?" the implication was again a damaging indictment of George's good intentions. The insinuation was unmistakable that George might *want* her to "go through all this again." The climax of innuendo was reached when she wound up her wild exclamation with the outcry, "If *you don't* mind your own health, can't you at least *have some consideration* for me and the children?" This last sentence contained the unavoidable suggestion that George was careless of his own health and indifferent to the welfare of wife and children.

You may suspect here that I read into Edna's verbal barrage meanings and thoughts which are not hers. However, this is beside the point. The question is not what Edna's statements may mean to me. The more important question is how a husband with average sensitivity, acted on by his wife, will interpret the meaning of her words and actions.

The Meaning of an Act May Be Grasped, Understood, or Comprehended

The meaning of an act can be secured through (1) *superficial grasp*, (2) *deep understanding*, (3) *broad comprehension*. If I see a man approaching his neighbor, shaking his hand and saying, "How are you?" the man's motor behavior was perceived by my eyes and his speech behavior by my ears. The meaning of the act was then *grasped* in its superficial sensory aspects only. My eyes and ears merely registered the fact that a man greeted his neighbor and shook hands with him. Whether the handshake was prompted by friendship or mere courtesy; whether it was offered joyously or grudgingly, whether the greeting expressed genuine interest, formal politeness or wily hypocrisy, cannot be distinguished by means of sensory perception. Friendship and courtesy, genuine interest and hypocritical wile are motives, and motives cannot be seen or heard. Instead, they must be inferred, either by solid judgment or by vague intuition.

After the surface of the act has been explored by the senses, judgment or intuition penetrate *underneath* the superficial appearance and, thus, *understand* the motive. Understanding, therefore, goes deeper than mere sensory grasp. Whether understanding be based on solid judgment or vague intuition, in either case, it takes its cue from intonation, gestures and features. From these it infers the motives which are underneath or back of the act.

Articulate Behavior Is Grasped, Inarticulate Behavior Is Understood, Together They Are Comprehended

Motion and speech can be easily observed and measured in their details and, thereby, analyzed as to their precise meaning. A friendly handshake and a violent blow may be executed, at different times, by the same right arm of the same man. But the direction in which the arm swings, the force with which it is advanced, and the velocity with which it moves can be conveniently measured and shown to be different in the handshake from what they are in the blow. Moreover, the manner in which the muscles bend and stretch, pull and push, raise and lower the fingers and hands, forearm and upper arm in the various joints can again be measured and analyzed. Similarly with speech behavior. Words, sentences and paragraphs can be easily interpreted and analyzed in accordance with the rules of grammar, syntax and logic. This is different with intonations, gestures and features. Their analysis is either impossible or, at any rate, beyond the grasp of the average person. For some reason which it would be too difficult to explain here, behavior which is easily analyzed is called *articulate,* while behavior which defies analysis is termed *inarticulate.* We conclude that an act of behavior can be given articulate expression in motor and varied reactions, and inarticulate expression in tones, gestures and features. Articulate behavior is grasped by the senses, inarticulate behavior through judgment and intuition.

When the man whom I observed approaching his neighbor extended his right arm and asked, "How are you?" his handshake and inquiry were expressions of articulate behavior, motor and verbal. Its meaning could be analyzed through the senses as a greeting between two neighbors. In the ensuing conversation, I noticed a shadow of resentment in the knit brows and a strange tenseness in the taut cheeks. The man's look was staring and his smile wry and forced. While speaking his fingers fidgeted nervously about his coat and the arms executed gestures of impatience. His utterances had sharp undertones and shrill emphasis. All of this was inarticulate behavior. From it I inferred that the motive which prompted the encounter was not sheer joy of seeing the neighbor nor friendly interest. The precise motive of the act was not yet fully understood, but some motivational possibilities were already ruled out. After I had, thus, grasped the *articulate* portion of his reaction through my senses and its *inarticulate* portion through my intuitive judgment, I felt I had comprehended the total behavior through a synthesis of grasp and understanding.

Relatives Must Avoid Discrepency Between Articulate and Inarticulate Behavior

We shall now return to Edna. She gave articulate expression to her concern and devotion in verbal and motor reactions. This George grasped as a tendency toward marital service. At the same time, however, she gave inarticulate expression to her impatience and annoyance in tones, gestures, and features. This George understood as a disposition to marital domination. What George grasped in one portion of Edna's behavior clashed with what he understood in the other portion, and the result was that he failed to comprehend the meaning of her total behavior.

If a person notices that the articulate reactions of his friend, wife, father or mother clash with their inarticulate responses, he is likely to conclude that the clash is the result of hypocrisy and duplicity. He is then irritated, disappointed or repelled. This is the reason why it is so important for you relatives of patients to avoid a discrepancy between the articulate and inarticulate portions of your behavior. You must make every effort to regulate your conduct in such a manner that the returned patient will not be shocked by the observation that what he grasps in your motor and verbal reactions is contradicted by what he is made to understand in your intonations, gestures and features. If you do not avoid this duplicity of expression your son or husband will be unable to comprehend your total attitude and will become distrustful, perplexed and unhappy. The unhappiness will result from the realization that there is no common ground of understanding between him and his family. It is the sad lot of many of our patients that, after their return, they meet with a lack of understanding which they are unable to comprehend.

The Disease Mobilized the Patient's Sensitiveness to Inarticulate Behavior

There are sensitive and dull people. The dull react mainly to articulate behavior. Since the average individual is civil and courteous in matters of articulate speech and action, the dull have no difficulty escaping hurts and injuries. The sensitive are in a more precarious plight. They pay little attention to that portion of conduct which is expressed in words and motor action. Their attention is mainly focused on inarticulate responses. Raucous tones and hard features are apt to upset their countenance no matter how sweet the words and smooth the movements. And it is worth remembering that the patient who returns after months of agonizing loneliness is by no means dull. The disease has mobilized his sensibilities, and the anticipation of a stigmatized existence has sharpened his idiosyncrasies. This returned patient is particularly likely to listen to intonations, to scan features and to be hurt or even crushed if they are severe, reprimanding and disdainful. In my forthcoming lectures I shall make an effort to show how inarticulate intonations, gestures and features can be controlled to the point of harmonizing them with the words and motions of articulate behavior. Unless you produce this harmony between the two portions of your conduct, you will not be equal to the task of giving the proper after-care to your returned relative.

The lecture on the "major motives of behavior" is undoubtedly in theme and language above the educational level of the average ex-patient and his relatives. It treats the listener to such semi-technical terms as "dynamic habits," "extreme motivations," "sensory perception" and "inarticulate expression." In other words, the physician spoke up to the public, not down to it. Moreover, it must not be forgotten that the printed text is the result of marked revision in style and composition, differing considerably from the original spoken address. What is here compressed into one lecture was delivered in four separate installments spread over four consecutive biweekly meetings, each lasting from thirty to forty minutes. With so much time at his disposal the speaker had ample opportunity to enter into detail, to define terms and to explain meanings.

In presenting a list of lectures the author does not intend to offer a course in the art of public speaking of which he is by no means a master. At present it is merely intended to present themes and concepts. That the physician who wishes to become acquainted with the principles of group therapy must be able to address a group ought to be understood. If he is, he will have no difficulty making use of the ideas and formulations contained in each lecture no matter how compact and concentrated they may be. Nevertheless, the author does not wish to underestimate the gravity of the task. Group therapy is by no means an easy undertaking, and even the most careful study of this volume will hardly be likely to transform the reader into an expert. The writer has spent many years in assiduous practice before he acquired his present facility.

It is the writer's opinion that if the subjects of temper control and will training are to be emphasized in group procedures the discussions must move on as high a level of relevance and pertinence as possible. The listener must be made to realize that the meaning of his actions is "concealed in words and acts but revealed in tone, gesture and feature." He must be given adequate insight into what is direct expression and indirect implication of his daily performance. The topics of intentions, suggestions, insinuations and innuendo must be brought to his attention. He must be taught to watch and inspect his own inarticulate behavior which must be understood in contrast with his articulate utterance which must merely be grasped. Such instruction may seem difficult of formulation but the author found that it is feasible and attainable. Group therapy is a necessity. That it is also a difficulty is a credit to the method and a challenge to the physican.

LECTURE 5

THE TEMPERAMENTAL DEADLOCK

In one of my lectures I told you that behavior in a group is determined by two major motives, domination and service. I also told you that both motives are powerfully operative in every person and added that if they are to remain in a "healthy balance" the motive of service must have the edge over that of domination.*

Motives Move Muscles

A motive moves, and what it moves are muscles. This is a fundamental truth no matter how commonplace it sounds. Mark this statement: men act on one another through muscles mainly. And whether their actions be motivated by the spirit of service or that of domination the motive is carried out by muscular movement. Another thing must be kept in mind: what is irritating and annoying, insulting and agonizing is again behavior expressed in muscular action. Behavior, expressed through glands (sweating) or through blood vessels (blushing, blanching) will hardly ever have an irritating or offending effect.

Take a simple example, one that plays on the trivial plane of everyday existence. After a strenuous day's work a husband returns home. Previous to leaving the office he

*The writer is well aware of the existence of motives that have little or no relation to either of these "major motives." Behavior may be motivated by such essentially asocial urges as hunger, joy of recreation, curiosity, or interest in one's own health. These motives are largely individualistic and may be practiced apart from group aims. However, should they attain the status of group motives they would instantly assume the character of either service to or domination of the group, or any combination of the two trends. If recreation consists of a lonely swim it will hardly touch on group life. If the swimming is done in connection with a group it will be performed in the spirit of co-operative service or of competitive domination.

59

telephoned to tell his wife that he expected to arrive in about half an hour, adding that having an important evening engagement he wished to have an early dinner. On entering the dining room he notices the table is not set. He is piqued, disappointed, provoked. "What's the use of my telephoning?" he blurts out, "If that's the way I am treated I may as well eat outside." The wife apologizes meekly, protesting that the meal would have been ready in time had the husband called just a trifle earlier; even so, why fuss about a few minutes' delay? There is an angry reply, thundering and fuming on the part of the irate husband, mute resentment on the part of the flustered wife; the one indignant, the other crushed, both upset. The meal is finally taken in a tense atmosphere of strain, discomfort and irritation.

In this instance the husband's temper was aroused. What had actually happened was that his tendency to dominate was frustrated. The frustration mobilized hostile impulses which were given expression in muscular movements of the speech organs. Could the temper have been checked, the impulse restrained, the muscular expression prevented?

That muscular movements can be restrained, checked and stopped at will goes without saying. This ought to be sufficient to establish it as a principle that domineering behavior must never reach the state of muscular violence, either in speech (profanity) or in motion (blows). That tempers can be checked and dispositions changed was discussed on a previous occasion. I told you that the problem adult does precisely this checking and changing when, meeting strangers, he puts forward his best behavior. This observation alone ought to dispose of the time-worn argument that "after all you can't change a man's nature." In a phrase of this kind, temperament is thought of as identical with nature. I grant that it would be difficult to change a person's nature. But a man's temper is by no means his nature. At any rate, the average man's temper is not necessarily derived from natural inheritance. It is a far safer assumption that it is acquired through a process of mis-education.

"Nature" Can Be Changed Through Enforcement of Conditional Standard

Time was when it was considered "natural" that a father caned and strapped his children. In those days the father who lost his temper was perhaps not commended for his rash actions but his cruelty was excused as being ordained "by nature." When later public opinion turned against mistreatment of children fathers changed their "nature." How was it possible to change paternal "nature?" The answer is: by a change in public opinion.

Few persons dare give way to their "nature" if it runs counter to public opinion. You remember what I told you about the conditional standard. I said that it "determines which acts of behavior are called-for or uncalled-for by the requirements of time, place and circumstances of a given situation." I may add that public opinion determines which tenets of the conditional standard must be enforced, and which can be flouted.

In days bygone, public opinion tolerated wife beating and cruelty to children and animals. The result was that husbands, fathers and drivers who were so disposed yielded to their "nature" and indulged in orgies of cruelty. Today, when public opinion has definitely determined that cruelty to defenseless creatures is uncalled-for by the circumstances of civilized life, husbands, fathers and drivers seem to have discovered that their "nature" contains an unexpected strain of kindness.

Domestic Cruelty Can Be Outlawed by Determined Public Opinion

The husband who, in our example, did not refrain from bullying his wife when dinner was delayed a few minutes, did so because that portion of the conditional standard which declares bullying as uncalled-for is not enforced by present day public opinion. That same husband is expert in restraining his domineering "nature" where public opinion interposes its unequivocal disapproval. Public opinion condemns temper outbursts at social functions or in the presence of strangers anywhere. The consequence is that the average bully shelves his "nature" when he appears in public. This is a common observation which demonstrates that "nature" cannot only be changed but discarded with ease if it runs the danger of unqualified public condemnation.

There is a surprisingly large number of domestic bullies in the list of the parents, husbands and wives of our patients. Some display their temper in free explosion, others are more subtle and conceal it behind transparent invective or crafty innuendo. The present lectures are intended to teach you how to control your tempers, how to avoid invective and innuendo. But there ought to be little need for teaching. Anyone of you who is possessed of a propensity for bullying knows how to control the tendency, for instance, when you attend a party. Should public opinion decide to outlaw domestic cruelty everyone of you would instantly drop your bullying and domineering ways for fear of social ostracism. There would be no necessity for teaching you how to do it. You would change your disposition with the same ease with which you change you attitude when you enter the room of your hostess.

Lax Enforcement of Conditional Standard Encourages Domestic Bully

How can public opinion be changed? How can the public be induced to ostracize parental domination, marital bullying and any other kind of domestic cruelty?

The task seems super-human. Yet, at the risk of being ridiculed as a visionary I am ready to state that it is easy to accomplish. Of course, it would be difficult, although by no means impossible to change the views and standards of the general population. The millions of inhabitants of this country will hardly be inclined to accept your or my dictates. But don't forget that your public is not that of the United States. Your public consists of the relatively small circle of friends and associates with whom you entertain close contact. When you meet me I am your present public. At that moment you are subject to my scrutiny and my judgment. On meeting me you try to avoid creating a poor impression, and initiate a vigorous attempt to gain my approval for what you say or do. For the moment I am your public opinion. The question is whether I, as the present representative of public opinion, am pledged to a rigid enforcement of the conditional standard. If I am you will make every effort to conform with that standard, not only in words and acts, but also in implications. The calamity is that my method of enforcing the conditional standard may be lax. Then you may, for instance, tell me how yesterday you lost your temper with your wife and conclude your account with the casual statement, "It's too bad that I have to act that way. But I can't help it. I am a hard-working man, and when I come home from the shop I think I am entitled to an hour's rest. Don't you think I am right?" When you told me your story and added the concluding question I should have replied in the negative. You were not right. Indeed, you were very wrong. What happened was that, on arriving home, you found two neighbor women chatting with your wife. You were tired and in a mood to stretch out on the sofa and were prevented from doing so by the presence of the neighbors. After they I left you made a scene and precipitated a violent argument. Whether you are right or wrong is an irrelevant question. Even if you were right in claiming an hour's rest you were utterly wrong in permitting yourself to lose your temper. This is what I ought to have told you. If I had done so you would have been rebuked for your rude behavior. Public opinion, as represented by me, would have condemned your bullying tendency. Had I been a true defender of or contender for the conditional standard I would not even have dignified you by an explicit rebuff. I would have simply stated, "Whether you are right or wrong is immaterial. Temper is a matter of breeding, not of right and wrong." If you were possessed of even a modicum of finesse, the implied refutation would not have escaped you.

Recovery, Inc. Could Create Its Own Public Opinion

It is my sad duty to admit that I am a poor representative of public opinion. Under the present circumstances. I cannot get myself to express or indicate my disapproval of people who fail to control their tempers because they think they have a right to release them. Most likely my failure to rebuff domestic bullies is due to my fear of offending too many of my friends. However, I am determined to change tactics in my dealing with you relatives of our patients. I think it is about time to create within our group the type of public opinion that will set its face solidly against bullying and domineering no matter how skillful its disguise. It seems to me we should not hesitate to cultivate in our midst an attitude that will condemn all varieties of domestic cruelty with uncompromising severity. Then we will be the first group of numerical importance that will do away with that lethal blight of human relations: the dual conditional standard which prohibits rudeness outside the family circle and sanctions or at least tolerates it inside the home. We, the members of the Recovery, Inc. group, have pioneered in so many ways. Why not pioneer in matters of domestic adjustment? Why should we not try to create our own brand of public opinion?

The average person cannot withstand the pressure of

public opinion within the group to which he belongs. Of course, there are the hobos and Bohemians. They seem to do as they please and fail to conform to a set standard. But then, they do not belong to a settled group. The average man and woman belong to a well-ordered group and depend on its public opinion, provided it is enforced. When years ago public opinion could·not be enlisted for the support of the Volstead Act the latter was unenforceable; at the same time, the Harrison narcotic law was successfully enforced because it had the endorsement of public opinion. Let public opinion be unequivocally opposed to the divorce evil and it will be reduced to its unavoidable minimum. Let it set its face unqualifiedly against criminal tendencies and crime will be relegated to the outer fringe of society instead of permeating it close to its core.

Argumentative Temper Is Common Among Relatives of Patients

I quoted the example of the husband who returned home and fumed because dinner was not ready. I added the story of the man who went into a rage because his wife had the "effrontery" to chat with neighbors at an inopportune time. Obviously, the two temperamental persons had hardly any excuse for exploding. You may now contrast the reactions of these gentlemen with the behavior of our prototype of a domestic temper—Edna.

Edna was subtle. She did not explode, she did not raise her voice to the pitch of yelling, nor did she bang doors or pound her fist on the table. As I said, Edna was civilized, and her method of matrimonial domination made use of approved means. Her chief weapons were: argument and criticism. Compare her behavior with that of the two explosive men, and you will realize that they used vocal and verbal violence while Edna used vocal and verbal strategy. The two men tried to outshout their wives, Edna made an effort to convince her husband that she was right and he was wrong, that she knew how to do things and he did not.

I know that some of you relatives of patients are given to violent explosions. However, it is merely your voice and your vocabulary that explode. I have yet to hear of the husband, father or mother of a returned patient who exploded to the point of using muscular violence in their temper outbreaks. Most of you, it seems to me, are of the Edna type. You scorn brutality and make use of strategy—the strategy of the argument. Be this as it may, my estimate is that the violent temper is practically nonexistent, the explosive temper relatively rare, and the argumentative temper quite common among the relatives of our patients.

Edna's Argumentative Temper Led to "Tempermental Deadlock"

Edna had an argumentative temper which grated on George's sensitive ears. She made a show of superiority whenever an opportunity offered. She was, of course, a consummate "back seat driver" and reprimanded George for driving too slowly or too fast, for passing a light or not passing it in time. More irritating was her inveterate habit of correcting George when he made an innocent statement. He might be reading the paper and venture a comment on some news item. Instantly she interrupted him with the exclamation, "How can you say that? That's the way you always talk. Can't you ever use your brain?" In such verbal scrimmages it was the subtle use of the words "always" and "ever" that conveyed the hidden implication of a wholesale condemnation of George's intellectual capacity. George was just a child and "always" wrong; Edna had a mature mind and was "ever" right. She was most agonizing when she criticized and corrected him in the presence of visitors. He offered an opinion and was rebuked by her shrill outcry, "But honey, that is not so. I don't understand how anybody can make such a statement." George usually kept his peace and consoled himself with the realization that "after all, it is her nature." But occasionally, especially when the argument developed in the privacy of the home, he could not contain himself and flung back a sharp answer. Then Edna let loose and poured forth an endless stream of criticisms and accusations. A major contest was on and disturbed domestic peace in an ugly torrent of recriminations and countercharges.

You may be inclined to dismiss my account of Edna's and George's squabbles as just so many trivialities. But then, don't forget that we are engaged in a discussion of average everyday adjustment. And keep in mind that everyday adjustment means adjustment to trivialities. Domestic life, at any rate, consists of hardly anything but trivial occurrences. Whenever you find irreparable rifts and unabridged dissension among close relatives be certain they took their inception, in nine cases out of ten, from just those trivial irritations which I described as the source of Edna's and George's daily struggle. Remember what I told you weeks ago: "What taxes the adjustive capacity of the average individual are the more or less continuous, repetitious and habitual irritations of common everyday life. Calamities and disasters are hardly ever habitual; small irritations frequently are." (page 40) Edna's tendency to criticize, correct and argue about George's behavior was repetitious, habitual and well nigh continuous; gradually it developed into an "argumentative temper." She was bitter and resented George's "stubbornness," brooded over his "obviously willful" opposition and saw nothing but spite and obstinacy in his refusal to bow to her dictates. In time she reached the stage, so common in marital warfare, when she expected George to be stubborn and recalcitrant and anticipated opposition and refusals. George's mere presence was now irritating to her. Expecting opposition, she was always ready to fight it. Her mood was that of a constant preparedness for sallies and parries. The same tendency to expect trouble and to be prepared to fight it began to possess George. The atmosphere was charged with a sullen spirit of bellicosity, an innocent remarks and meaningless gestures were sufficient to precipitate an outbreak. One day George returned home and, for some reason, forgot to close the door. The following dialogue took place:

Edna: What's the idea of leaving the door open?

George: Why do you ask such a question?

Edna: Can't I ask questions any more?

George: I am sick and tired of your silly questions.

Edna's and George's temperaments had obviously locked horns, and their marital relations turned into what may be called a "temperamental deadlock."

The Habit of Experiencing Neutral Event of Irritating Leads to "Temperamental Tangle"

Ever since the formation of Recovery, Inc., the Association of Former Patients, there was a constantly increasing trek of relatives to my office. The problems raised by the Association had weighed heavily on their consciences. They came and unburdened themselves, sometimes tearfully, sometimes defiantly. Many asked advice and guidance, others sought exoneration. All of them had become ruefully aware of the shaky nature of their domestic adjustment. Whatever were their motives, their complaints, protestations and entreaties gave me a welcome insight into the average home situation of our patients. I was surprised to see how many of them lived in the atmosphere of the "temperamental deadlock." The popular conception of the home as the seat of peace and partnership seemed to resolve itself into a romantic vision. Realistic observation tore the dream apart and revealed a scene dominated by fierce rivalry and a ruthless attempt to subjugate the partner. It would be an unfair generalization to claim that the "temperamental deadlock" is characteristic of all families of our patients. However, few of them offer the picture of even relative domestic harmony; most of them suffer from some degree of temperamental tangle.

Some time ago I gave you a graphic description of the dynamics of average misbehavior. You remember I told you that events produce experiences, that experiences give rise to impulses and that impulses release acts of behavior. I summed up by stating that "in adjusted behavior, a hostile event produces an irritating experience, it then gives rise to a hostile impulse and releases a hostile act. A neutral event produces a neutral experience, a neutral impulse, and, finally, a neutral act. A friendly event results in a stimulating experience, a friendly impulse and friendly act." (See page 28) You may now analyze the "temperamental deadlock" in terms of event, experience, impulse and act. When dinner was delayed in the case of the returning husband, the event was trivial, insignificant and neutral. It ought to have produced the neutral experience of having to wait a few minutes. Instead, there was an experience of extreme irritation with the resulting hostile impulse and hostile act. Similarly with the neighbor women occupying the coveted sofa and George forgetting to close the door. In all these instances, a neutral event was experienced as irritating, and the irritation precipitated a sequence of hostile impulses and reactions. Obviously, if the victims of the "temperamental deadlock" should cease experiencing neutral events as irritating there would be little occasion for temper outbursts and none for a deadlock.

A "Healthy Balance" Is Established If the "Intellectual Appraisal" Predominates Over the "Emotional Expectation"

To experience an event is to interpret its meaning. This

is certainly true of consciously experienced events. Suppose a drop of rain falls on my cheek. I shall then interpret its meaning as being rain and not snow, as being the result of a drizzle and not of a cloudburst. If my interpretation is not carried any further the event stands analyzed by a process of *intellectual appraisal*. However. I may be inclined to add another interpretive step. I may surmise that the rain is likely to bring relief from a suffocating heat wave. Then I interpret the event as welcome and desirable. To the intellectual appraisal has now been added the *emotional expectation*.

The conditional standard demands that, in interpreting the meaning of a neutral event the intellectual appraisal takes the lead over the emotional expectation. Intellect and emotion are, then, in a state of "healthy balance." The balance is disturbed if in a neutral situation emotion is permitted to take the lead. We then speak of an "emotional imbalance." I told you that, after the development of the "temperamental deadlock," Edna expected George to be stubborn and anticipated opposition and refusals. Emotional expectation took the lead over intellectual appraisal in interpreting the meaning of neutral events which were then habitually experienced as irritating. The result was that hostile impulses were aroused and hostile acts released almost uninterruptedly.

A Healthy Balance of Experience Is Largely Dependent on Public Opinion

It ought to be clear now that adjustment depends on the manner in which events are experienced that is, interpreted. Interpretation will be correct if intellect and emotion are in a state of "healthy balance." This sounds simple enough. However, a "healthy balance" can be obtained only through persistent cultivation. What must be cultivated is the predominance, in neutral events, of intellectual appraisal over emotional expectation. A person who succeeds in cultivating this predominance establishes cultured methods of experiencing and interpreting events. It will now be easy for you to grasp a distinction which I made in a previous lecture when I called Edna merely civilized but not cultured. Culture refers to balancing of experiences, civilization to muscular control of impulses. Edna controlled her impulses but failed to balance her experiences. After the development of the "temperamental deadlock" she even had difficulty controlling her impulses.

The maintenance of balanced experiences depends to a large extent on the influence of public opinion. The precise nature of this interdependence will be discussed in subsequent lectures. For the present I merely mention that contemporary public opinion does little to discourage the "temperamental tangle" or to encourage the "healthy balance" in the management of domestic relations.

The indictment of present day public opinion is by no means a fortuitous utterance in the context of Lecture 5. On the contrary, it is a constituent part of Recovery, Inc. teaching. The public at large considers temper the legitimate offspring of "human nature" and thus declares it as unalterable and inaccessible to education as "nature itself." Recovery, Inc. rejects with vigor the claim to unalterability and brands uncontrolled temper as the illegitimate offspring of a public opinion oblivious to its duties and responsibilities. The vicious doctrine of the "irresistible impulse" the validity of which is under grave suspicion even in forensic cases, is part and parcel of the concept of temper as "natural" inheritance. To Recovery, Inc. heredity is no brief for an unrestrained laissez-faire attitude, and "nature" no carte blanche for domestic cruelty. Both patients and relatives are made to realize that the "nature" which they inherited is subject to the influence of training and self-discipline. In emphasizing the necessity for self-discipline the author does not intend to assume the function of a moralist or uplift crusader but to perform the plain duty of the physician whose pursuit is to cure effects by removing their causes. And many relapses have their undoubted cause in uncontrolled domestic temper. And many tempers can be traced back to the unfortunate doctrine of the "irresistible impulse." And the doctrine of irresistibility is sanctioned by a public opinion which is irresponsibly tolerant of temperamental misconduct.

LECTURE 6

THE "WRONG-FEARING" TEMPERAMENT

It is evening, and I am strolling in the park. The situation is one of calm and serenity. I am relaxed and my thoughts and feelings are in a state of equilibrium. All of a sudden, a shabbily-dressed man approaches me asking for money. The situation has now changed. An event has occurred which disturbs my equilibrium and forces me to take a position. I must decide whether or not to grant the plea. True enough, the decision is not important. But it carries with it the disturbing factor inherent in every decision: I may be right, or may be wrong.

Conflicts Disturb Equilibrium

A natural sympathetic urge bids me to be charitable. But another sentiment rises to defy my sense of humanity. It occurs to me that so many beggars accost me on the street and that my contribution to the relief of misery imposes some measure of privation on my own family. The *inclination* to help the stranger and the *obligation* to attend to the needs of my family compete for my consideration, and I am headed straight for a conflict. The conflict is of minor proportion but, nevertheless, a conflict, with its customary burning question: Am I right, or am I wrong?

You see, when prior to meeting the beggar I strolled along the winding paths, the question of right and wrong was absent from my mind. That's what made me feel relaxed. That's what gave equilibrium to my thought and feeling. Now that the question arises whether I am about to act correctly, my calm and serenity are gone, and my equilibrium is—gently—challenged. My mind is soon made up, and I decide to part with the coin. The stranger leaves and I continue the stroll. After a few steps I notice that my poise does not return. The man's image is before my mind. I remember his features, and in recollection they seem to reflect the coarse expression of a hardened professional rather than the mellowed lines of a distressed sufferer. I am in a conflict again. Was it, after all, wrong to have offered the assistance? Was I tricked by an undeserving "racketeer?" Why, just recently I read about the "beggar racket" that infests the city. And now I remember occasions when I made charitable offerings only to see the recipient instantly entering a tavern presumably to spend my money on drinks. Was my action wrong after all? Did I perchance help an unworthy individual continue his unworthy conduct? These and similar questions crowd my brain, and they work with the intensity of a painful conflict, and my equilibrium is again—this time harshly—challenged.

Conflicts Unresolved by Decision Create Dilemma

Life is full of conflicts. You are anxious to own an automobile but hesitate to buy it because the money should by right be reserved for the purchase of a home. You are weary and desirous of spending a restful day at home, but it would be wrong to neglect your business or professional duty. These are simple examples of everyday conflicts and their common feature is that *personal inclination* pulls you one way and *group obligation* the other. You are torn between the two trends the one of which is considered "wrong," the other "right." The "wrong" trend beckons and tempts and promises pleasure or relaxation or relief; the "right" trend warns and commands and promises a strengthening of your self-respect. The conflict can be solved by a decision only. But frequently a decision is not easy. Your friend is in need and appeals to you for help. However, your means are limited and your family has a prior claim. If you follow the call of friendship you may be disloyal to your family. If you heed the plea of your family, you may violate the code of friendship. The conflict is here not one between an inclination and an obligation but rather one between two obligations. A decision may be and frequently is impossible. This situation is what is called a *dilemma*. If the dilemma continues, you may spend days and weeks in suspense and indecision, anxious to do what is right and to avoid what is wrong, but unable to determine which way to turn. The result will be an abiding inability to relax, or a *sustained tenseness*. Mark it: whenever you do not know whether you are right or wrong you are bound to be tense.

Conflicts and Dilemmas Cause Emotional Turmoil

There are countless varieties of conflicts and any of them may develop into a long drawn out, vexing dilemma. Your cough has troubled you for a week. If it is nothing but a trifling irritation, it may be extravagance to consult a physician. But what if it is the first sign of tuberculosis? Or, the baby has a slight elevation of temperature. Should the doctor be summoned, or can you afford to wait and save the expense? These situations are commonplace enough. Yet, once they arise they throw you into an emotional turmoil. You do not know which course to follow. You rack your brain in order to find the proper solution; you are anxious to avoid a mistake and are painfully aware that should you take a wrong step the consequences may be grave.

In some conflicts no serious consequences can reasonably be expected. Yet, the commotion and agitation they may produce are bound to play havoc with your peace of mind. Your employer is a jovial, kindly gentleman but has for years neglected to increase your salary. It would be easy to petition for a raise. It may be refused, but the well-tried humanity of your superior is a sure guarantee that no other consequences need be feared but the denial of your request.

Nevertheless, you cannot muster the courage to "speak up." For months and years your wife urges you to make the necessary effort; she pleads with you, appeals to your conscience, invokes the specter of future insecurity, inveighs against your cowardice, but all to no avail. You simply cannot, for some obscure reason, assert yourself in this matter. The dilemma which is the inevitable result saps your self-confidence, gives you a sense of insufficiency, and creates a state of—tenseness.

I could here quote the tragicomical but agonizing complications which trouble your mind when some ludicrous questions of social etiquette are at issue: to accept, ignore, or refuse an invitation: to be on time, or a trifle late, or a few minutes early at a social engagement? To wear formal or informal dress? What is involved in such "pseudo-conflicts" is not fear of practical consequences but some absurd and irrational sensitiveness to other peoples' opinions. Yet, the result is again: fear of being wrong, disturbance of equilibrium, commotion, unrest, and—tenseness

Life Would Be Peaceful But for the Question of "Right" and "Wrong"

But for that most annoying and peace-disturbing question of "right and wrong" life might be eternally calm and peaceful and devoid of tenseness. It is the absence of consideration for rightness and wrongness that gives infant behavior that fascinating touch of charm and innocence. Infants merely act but do not trouble to inquire whether their activity conforms to or deviates from a standard of correctness. Children are as a rule delightfully unconcerned about the rationality of their incentives and the consequences of their decisions. Provided they remain childlike, they do not stop to question the adequacy or inadequacy of their motives and intentions. In other words, they do not "look into themselves," they are not *introspective*. This is different with adult persons. At every step before, during, and after performing an act they search their intentions, scrutinize their motives, and question the justification of their conduct. To be sure, there are dull people who are relatively free from introspection and lucky to escape the snares of conflicts and the pitfalls of tenseness. But the average individual is invariably a victim of his bend for introspection. He is sensitive to the problem of "right" and "wrong" and forever searching his soul and questioning the correctness of his behavior. Dullness makes for sterile equilibrium, sensitivity for moving conflicts.

Every conflict may develop into a dilemma. I told you that if you want to buy an automobile but need the money for your family that conflict can be solved by a decision. As a conscientious father you know that it is wrong to jeopardize the family budget and decide that the car must not be purchased. However, things are not always as simple as that. Suppose your children raise a clamor that everybody in the neighborhood has an automobile, that their social status is inferior because of the old-fashioned habits of their parents; suppose they quote authoritative statements of teachers, lecturers, and other representatives of public opinion to the effect that "spending is good investment"; that the maintenance of a low standard of living is contrary to the interests of the nation as a whole; that it jeopardized the social status of the children; that it is important to "keep abreast of the time"; suppose that in the end your wife who previously supported you begins to waver and is inclined to side with your children. You are no longer in a mere conflict but in a dilemma. Conscientiousness and sense of responsibility will not be of much help in this difficult situation. If your children's arguments are valid it might be counter to conscience and responsibility not to buy the car. It may be utterly wrong to save the money for the purchase of the home. How are you to act in this wretched dilemma? What is right? What is wrong?

The Sense of Being "Wrong" Leads to the Claims to Be "Right"

Forever afraid of being wrong, a conflict-torn or dilemma-plagued individual is anxious to convince himself that, in actual fact, he is right. This becomes his absorbing life task. You remember that what was most irritating to George was Edna's continual insistence that she was right and George wrong, that she knew how to do things and he did not. Edna was a woman with a sensitive soul, hence, bound to get into conflicts and dilemmas. As every bearer of tense conflicts she developed a passion for proving to herself that, indeed, she was not wrong. The most effective method of establishing one's claim to being right is a stubborn insistence on being listened to, on getting one's suggestions accepted and one's dictates acted on. This secures a sense of mastery and disposes, for the moment, of the suspicion of one's being wrong. Persons embroiled in perpetual inner conflicts are, therefore, eager to gain mastery over the partner. The common tendency to be domineering has here its root. It begins with the sense of being wrong, proceeds to the claim to be right, and ends in the overwhelming desire to dominate each and every situation. If the urge to dominate follows this pattern of bluntly imposing one's will on others it gives rise to the character type of the bully. The bullying husband and the bullying employer have both undergone this irresistible and relentless evolution from the sense of being wrong over the claim to be right to the grim determination to enforce one's will to mastery.

Service and Domination Are Mechanisms of Giving or Denying "Rights"

Life must be mastered and requires proper tools with which to overcome its difficulties. Such tools are called *mechanisms*. The mechanism of swimming masters the resistance of the waves, the mechanism of jumping masters that of height. Other examples of mechanisms are the lever and pulley which master the obstacle of loads and weights. You will now understand that what we call mechanisms are tools to overcome resistance. Group life calls for similar mechanisms or tools with which to master the task of living together. The two mechanisms which govern group life were discussed in previous lectures. They are: service and domination. Service is essentially the willingness to let others have their "rights" while domination is rooted in the insistence on the other person being "wrong." Bullying and tyrannizing are domination mechanisms; submissiveness, coyness, thoughtfulness, and consideration are service mechanisms. A sensitive woman of the Edna type will shrink from employing such a crude tool as bullying. As I told you repeatedly, Edna was subtle, and if she was determined to exercise mastery be certain the mechanisms which she used were subtly chosen. They were: criticism, sarcasm, innuendo, plain debate, and persuasion. What the bully gains by means of crude *violence* the Edna type achieves through the mechanism of clever argumentation and shrewd *strategy*.

Insistence on Being "Right" Disturbs Adjustment

Whenever two people meet they form a group. The group may be that of a casual acquaintance or of a lasting friendship or of a lifelong marital union. Two people can never be expected to have identically the same opinions, habits, likes, and tastes. If they are to live in peace they must evolve mechanisms for adjusting their differences and difficulties. How can difficulties be adjusted if one partner always insists on being right? If the abiding sense of being wrong drives the conflict-burdened individual to force his "right" views and "right" demands on his partner, adjustment must of necessity fail.

Too many of our discharged patients are forced to live in homes where mothers, fathers, sisters and brothers continually insist on being "right" and employ either the mechanism of bullying or that of subtle strategy to enforce their "rights." During the past several years when my responsibilities as officer of Recovery, Inc., the Association of Former Patients, brought me in frequent personal contact with you relatives, I was startled by the vehemence with which you currently emphasized your being right and your son or daughter being wrong. It was a common experience that a parent recounted some incident of domestic friction and wound up with the dramatic exclamation, "Don't you think I was right?" In the past few months I adopted the rule to return the stock reply, which I quoted to you already, "Whether you are right or wrong is immaterial. Temper is a matter of breeding, not of right and wrong." (See page 64)

Conflicts Explain Poor Manners But Do Not Excuse Them

Persons of "good breeding" are by no means free from conflicts, but in an effort to solve them they refrain from employing the mechanisms of domination. They have been "bred to the manner" of service, and in the process of breeding they evolved the mechanisms of "good manners." Do you realize that your domestic problems are matter of "manners?" Manners can be changed, revised, and corrected; poor manners can be discarded and good ones adopted.

Everybody suffers from deep-seated conflicts. But it is not true that everybody has poor manners. In other words, the presence of conflicts is no valid excuse for bad behavior and poor adjustment. Conflicts *explain* temper but do not *excuse* it. Of late when public clamor for popular education gained momentum treatises on conflicts and how to treat them were poured into a perplexed public hungry for information. These popular treatises gave currency to the widespread belief that conflicts must be dealt with by a medical or psychological authority. The individual was declared a helpless victim, and relief was available only at the hands of the expert. This is undoubtedly true of conflicts that ultimately lead to morbid behavior, to hysterical spells, compulsions, anxieties, and phobias. But what has *exceptional* conduct of this kind to do with *average* behavior? The average conflict which does not lead to disrupting symptoms requires no expert intervention. What it requires is the realization that one's manners are poor and the solid determination to mend them.

Poor Manners Are Maintained by the Premium of Pleasure Placed on Them

Poor manners are maintained and cultivated into set habits because they *suit* and *please* the ill-mannered person. The pronouncement may strike you as unwarranted exaggeration, but I shall have no difficulty proving to you that I do not overstate. Just remember your last experience when you had a "just" cause for criticizing your neighbor. You talked about her to a close friend. In other words, you gossiped. Remember how on this occasion you did not merely voice your disapproval but persisted in repeating over and again how utterly "wrong" was the neighbor's attitude, how distorted her views, how silly her statements? You fairly revelled in scoring her faults and weaknesses and ripped unsparingly into her character and reputation. Indeed, if you only care to recall, you will remember that you indulged in gross misstatements in spite of the fact that misstating is otherwise not your custom. And, withal, that neighbor is not your enemy. You do not even dislike her. Indeed, she is a friend of yours, and you enjoy her company and admire many of her features. Nevertheless, at the time of your gossiping spree, you felt impelled to speak of her with venom. You did so because as an individual with a fair degree of sensitiveness you fairly burst with conflicts. They harass you with the sense of being wrong and drive you with elemental force to prove to yourself that not you but others are wrong. In order to be convincing you'd better lay on heavily and paint the victims of your criticism with such abysmally black colors that, in comparison, the gray of your own "wrong" soul must needs appear white. I do not have to tell you that gossip of this kind is a common occupation, indeed, a very favorite pastime. Its objective is to inveigh against the moral character of the one tattled about, not so much in order to "knock" the other one but rather to "boost" one's own conflict-shaken ego. Be certain that when you indulged in the "poor manners" of gossiping the habit *suited* your temper and *pleased* your conflict—ridden self. Moreover, if you are honest with yourself you will admit that the act of gossiping provides you with a rare thrill that you would not like to miss. From this you will learn that "poor manners" are persistently cultivated and permitted to crystallize into hardened habits because a premium of secret pleasure is placed on them.

Gossip is a mechanism capable of relieving the tenseness caused by conflicts. It gives relief by convincing you that the "other fellow" is wrong, so atrociously wrong that your failing in this respect must appear very small, indeed. Bullying, sarcasm, ridicule are other such mechanisms. They all tend to demonstrate the wrongness, weaknesss, helplessness, and inadequacy of others. After bullying, ridiculing, or reprimanding others you have the doubtful distinction of having scored a victory. It is this sense of being victorious that gives you the pleasure of which I spoke when I stated that poor manners are cultivated and permitted to become set habits "because a premium of 'secret' pleasure is placed on them."

Edna's Conflict Sensitiveness Was Due to Her "Wrong-Fearing" Temperament

The man of breeding has been trained to secure satisfaction from subduing his own inclination. He scorns the pleasure derived from bullying or imposing on others. Moreover, the man of breeding while desiring to do right is not afraid—in daily trivialities—of being wrong. Hence he has no desire to prove that others are wrong. The result is that he is serene, genial, and conciliatory. You will perhaps here realize that what we called temper has also its main source in the perpetual desire to prove that the other person is wrong. Edna was the crowning example of a "wrong-fearing" temperament. I told you that as a typical "problem adult" she displayed her temper mainly at home and curbed it efficiently in outside contacts. In time she developed a ludicrous sensitiveness to the vexatious problem of "right" and "wrong." If George merely asked the innocent question, "Did you bring my suit to the tailor?" she was likely to snap back, "What makes you think I forget everything? I am not an idiot." The simple inquiry suggested to her the suspicion that George might think of her as forgetful, as being deficient in memory, as being—"in the wrong." The perpetual fear of being wrong was forever in conflict with the overpowering desire to be right and created an intense *conflict sensitiveness*. The sensitiveness made her so irritable that explosions followed one another almost uninterruptedly. Each explosion gave her an instantaneous, short-lived "secret" pleasure from putting George "in his place." He was wrong, and she won't let him "get away with it."

Well-Bred Persons Have a Sense of Humor, Ill-Mannered Persons Lack It

I told you that tempers and dispositions can be changed provided the one displaying them (1) acquires *insight* and realizes the need for a change of manners, (2) is inspired with the determination to effect the necessary change (page 51). Had Edna been able to realize that her temper tantrums had for their sole objective the desire to enjoy the spurious pleasure of seeing George "in the wrong" she might have begun to laugh at so absurd an aim. To be able to laugh at a thing means to refuse to take it seriously. The trouble with the ill-bred individual is that he takes his stirrings, his conflicts, and fears ridiculously seriously. The well-bred person has a sense of humor; the ill-mannered person lacks it. I hope that these lectures will make it possible for you to laugh at your paltry conflicts, to smile at your fear of not being right, and to joke at your urge to prove others wrong. If you manage to do that your conflicts, fears and apprehensions will be relieved, and the recovered patient will return to a home pervaded by the spirit of patience and forbearance and a—sense of humor.

The physician must have a consistent viewpoint of behavior and adjustment. If he is to guide his patients and their relatives, he must have the average qualities of the leader and teacher, i.e., he must be as certain of his views as is humanly possible. What he must avoid is self-contradiction and uncertainty. The consistent viewpoint will safeguard him against both handicaps. He may have at his command a properly integrated viewpoint of his own. Then, he may disregard all the lectures presented in this volume. If he lacks a system of well-organized opinions, he will be adequately guided by the views and notions offered by the author. They passed through the crucible of many years of practical experience and stood the test of successful practical application.

At this point it is already apparent that the lectures follow a well-conceived pattern the details of which are clearly discernible. After outlining the general principles of constitution and environment in Lecture 1 the writer discussed the problems of after-care and illustrated by means of relevant case reports the responsibilities of the relatives for the home adjustment of the ex-patients. In Lecture 2 he stressed the importance of adjustment, control and balance, and chose the case of George and Edna as a broad basis for an elaboration of his views on domestic temper. He then traced the marital adjustment of the couple in its manifold phases, invariably focusing the listener's attention on the all-pervading significance of trivial everyday conduct. Through the introduction of a concrete case description he gained a vantage point from which theoretical subjects could be conveniently analyzed within the framework of a practical situation. This combination of concrete description and academic exposition proved an effective means of presentation.

LECTURE 7

TEMPER AND INSIGHT

Suppose you speak of a certain couple and state, "They have been *marrying* twenty years." You will instantly stop short and add apologetically, "I beg your pardon; what I meant to say was that they have been *married* twenty years." In this instance you made a mistake and immediately noticed the slip. How is it you made the discovery so quickly? Do you keep an incessant watch over your speech performance? Are you so self-conscious and introspective that you are continually on guard against errors?

Insight Is Acquired Through
Perpetual Self-Scrutiny

You may be a reasonably relaxed person and fairly free from the habit of morbid introspection; however, there is no doubt that, unbeknown to yourself, you are forever on the alert lest your reactions of speech, thought, and action fall short of accepted standards. If, for some reason, you exclaim inadvertently, "I am positively I am right," not a second will pass before you will be painfully aware of the mistake which you made when you used the adverb "positively" in place of the adjective "positive." The correction will follow automatically. Why do you hasten to correct the misstatement? The person who listened to you knew what you intended to express. The meaning of your sentence was clear even if your grammar was faulty. Why, then, the correction? The answer is: the average individual has a passion for being right and for avoiding being wrong.

The fact that people have the capacity for instant

correction of errors and slips proves that they are
continually watching their performances. This process of
perpetual self-scrutiny and self-inspection makes it
possible for them to gain and maintain *insight* into the
propriety, adequacy, and pertinency of their acts of
behavior.

When you made the mistake about a couple "marrying"
twenty years you offended against the standard of logic;
when you used "positively" instead of "positive" your
mistake was one of grammar. An individual with average
intelligence and average school knowledge masters these
standards to such an extent that he hardly ever violates
them. If violation occurs correction follows instantan-
eously. Insight or, as we may now say, the knowledge of
having made a mistake, works here with an almost 100
percent exactness.*

Insight Gives knowledge of Having
Offended Against a Standard

I told you repeatedly that when the recovered patient
returns home he is likely to suffer from the misbehavior of
his relatives. I also told you that misbehavior of the kind
that is likely to confront him is due to the common
disregard for the rules of the so-called "conditional
standard." In one of my lectures I said that the conditional
standard "refers to behavior which while ordinarily not
regulated by standards may, 'under certain conditions,'
become subject to regulation." I added the following
examples: "When at home I am permitted to dress or
undress as I choose. But 'conditions' change when I leave
the home. Then I *must* be dressed. Similarly at home I may
smoke; at a concert I *must not*. At home I may whistle,
sing, hum, and yawn but when interviewed by my

---

*Only that variety of insight is here considered which comes into operation *after* a
mistake was made. Essentially, this is what is commonly called "hind-sight." The other
variety of insight which goes by the name of "foresight" is here not discussed.

prospective employer the whistling, singing, humming, and yawning would inevitably be interpreted a improper conduct." (See page 37) At present I wish to resume the discussion of the conditional standard from the viewpoint of insight, i.e., the knowledge of having offended against a standard.

If you walk on the street it is immaterial whether you move close to or at a distance from the curb. There is no standard which regulates this portion of your street behavior. However, if you are in the company of a lady "conditions" change, and the "conditional standard" directs you to take your place between the curb and the lady. The rule has become so deeply grooved in your consciousness that you hardly ever fail to take your "correct" position. The conditional standard works here almost as automatically as do the standards of grammar and logic when you choose your words in a common conversation or your arguments in an ordinary discussion. Should it happen that, for some reason, you find yourself in the wrong position you will instantly step to the other side and perhaps apologize to your companion. Insight into your mistake will operate with promptness.

Let us now assume that the lady in question is not a stranger or friend but your wife. Will you now also immediately act on your insight if your position is contrary to the requirements of the standard? Will you then also hasten to change your position after discovering the mistake? I gave you the answer to this question when I discussed the behavior of the "problem adult" who is meticulous in his observance of the conditional standard in outside contacts but utterly remiss in his domestic conduct.

The "Problem Adult" Chooses Not to Exercise Insight at Home

The "problem adult" hardly ever bangs doors in the home of friends but may do that habitually in his own.

When invited he is eager to converse with his table partner, but at home he frequently maintains a stony silence toward his wife. Moreover, should he accidentally slam a door in the home of his friend or feel indisposed to carry on a conversation at his hostess' table he would instantly realize (or have insight into) the unseemliness of his conduct and offer an apology. Do you think his insight is keener abroad than at home? Is it logic to assume that one and the same person has excellent insight in one locality and almost none in another? This would be an absurd supposition, and the only possible conclusion is that the problem adult has good insight into his missteps both outside and inside the home but makes use of it in one of the spheres only. In his outside contacts he *chooses* to exercise his insight; in his domestic contacts he *chooses* not to exercise it.

If a husband has currently the poor taste to read the paper while he is sitting with his wife at the table his insight into the impropriety of the act is beyond reasonable doubt. He knows that his behavior is discourteous and excuses himself on the score of having the *right* to practice the discourtesy because the pressure of work leaves him no other time for reading the news. And, after all, a man must keep himself informed! You will instantly recall my statement that, in conflict-torn individuals, the "sense of being wrong" leads to the "claim to be right." (See page 78) That the claim is a flimsy excuse rather than a valid explanation is plain from the fact that, on numerous occasions, the "overworked" husband prefers to spend his precious time on a dime novel instead of on table conversation although the dime novel is hardly likely to quench his thirst for information. Obviously, that husband *chooses* to be discourteous. His misbehavior is not due to a lack of insight but to a failure or even refusal to practice it.

Premium of Pleasure Blocks Insight
Into Temperamental Misconduct

You have heard the remark that the temper of a given person is inborn and ingrained, that it is as unchangeable as are the proverbial leopard's spots. The husband who bangs doors or reads at supper time does so from temperamental leanings. Is it true that the inclination to make noise or to maintain an icy silence is as unchangeable as the leopard's spots? Of course, if a man thinks he has the *right* to indulge his inclinations the sense of being right adds relish to the reaction and places the premium of pleasure on it. And if a man secures from an act the pleasurable feeling of being right he will refuse to abandon it and *choose* to continue. But for the premium of pleasure that rests on temperamental behavior a change of temper would be as easy as a change in clothing. The obvious inference is that in order to make men control their tempers they must be made to realize that the claim to be right is no justification for the will to be rude.

After you finish dressing or eating you do not protest that you had a right to dress or eat. Under ordinary circumstances the propriety and justification of the act is not contested by any person or standard. You are not called upon to offer apologies or excuses for innocent behavior of this kind. Should, however, a person after consuming a meal, exclaim, "Don't you think I had a right to eat?" you would instantly know that the eater himself thought the propriety of his act might be challenged and had to be justified. Mark it: whenever a person insists on being right he either was or felt he was challenged. Or, whenever anybody insists on being right it is obvious he thought he was or might have been wrong. If you are convinced of the innocence of your behavior you do not apologize for it; you may draw the conclusion that the emphasis on one's being right indicates a sense of being wrong. In other words: whenever you claim to be right you display insight into being or thinking of being wrong. Self justification is a sequel either to self accusation or to the fear of outside challenge.* It will be well for you relatives of former patients to realize that your persistent claims to be right are a clear indication of your perpetual sense of being wrong.

Edna'a Insight Into Being Wrong Was Blocked by Determination to "Stand on Her Rights"

After the "temperamental deadlock" developed between Edna and George home life was a bedlam of squabbles and recriminations. The question of right and wrong was uppermost in the minds of both marital contestants. When one of them asked a harmless question the partner might retort temperamentally, "Why do you ask me that?" and provoke the tart counter question, "Haven't I a right to ask questions any more?" Domestic peace was gone, and resentment and bitterness took its place. In due time, both Edna and George became obsessed with the idea that they had to "stand on their rights" and must not permit "the other side" to neglect or infringe on them. Edna's motto was, "I'll force him to do his part." And with this program in mind she set out on a systematic campaign to make demands just in order to show George that he "can't get away with it." She had always done her shopping without assistance from her husband. Now she currently discovered that she had no time to visit the downtown stores and frequently telephoned George to do an errand or two for her after leaving his office. Gradually, the telephone requests became routine. To the shopping assignments were added other commissions. "Honey, couldn't you drop in at Elsa's on the way home and pick up a package she has for me?" As

---

*This formation about the claim to be right pointing to a sense of being wrong applies, of course, to trivial, everyday grievances only. It may also but does not have to hold in disputes about realistic rights, privileges, and possessions.

the demands increased George suspected a scheme and balked. He first offered excuses for not complying; finally, he bluntly refused. Edna was furious. Didn't she have a right to get cooperation? Her demands became more numerous and more insistent and George's refusals more abrupt and outspoken. The battle for rights raged along the entire length of the marital front. Differences of opinion and taste were no longer adjusted amicably but fought over ferociously.

Both Edna and George were what you would unhesitatingly call "nice people." Both subscribed to the standard of clean living and fair dealing; both had the capacity for kind feeling and sympathetic understanding. Nor were they grossly deficient in common sense and judgment. When Edna evolved her newly devised program of not "letting George get away with it" she had a clear understanding that the principle meant spite and vindictiveness and was likely to undermine domestic peace. There was no doubt in her mind that this "fight to the finish" might easily lead to the "finish." What she did was done with full insight into the undesirable and reprehensible nature of her conduct. But when the idea assailed her that her procedure might wreck her home she discarded it with the consideration that it would be wrong to let George "walk over her." You see, her insight into being wrong was sideswiped by her determination to "stand on her rights."

This is the crux of domestic discord in practically all its manifestations: one partner bullies the other and has the unobscured insight that bullying is indefensible. But the insight is without effect because it is swept aside by the self-deception that the bullying is done "by right." Do you see the involved tragedy? Humans are so constituted that they relish a "fight for rights." If they manage to convince themselves that their fight is one for "rights" the prospects are they will be reluctant to cease fighting and will *choose* to continue. The result will be the "temperamental deadlock."

Domestic Fights Center Around
Imaginary Issue of Being Right

There are occasions—rare in civilized groups—when men fight for *objective realities*. There are occasions when they are *really and objectively* assaulted and insulted. There are other occasions when vicious, scheming, unscrupulous persons attempt to gain an unfair advantage over them. Occasions of this kind call for fight. But that fight is, as a rule, fought coolly, deliberately, with slow moves and well-calculated measures. The impulsive outburst, the rise of temper, and sudden attack are, as a rule foreign to such realistic struggles. When parents conduct their temperamental domestic warfare against their sons, husbands against their wives, brothers against their sisters the fight is for something that has no reality except in the mind and imagination of the fighter. That something is the imaginary "sense of being right." I wish you would grasp this fundamental distinction: fights for realities are rare in the daily round of average life, and the fights encountered in domestic discord are almost invariably centered around the imaginary issue of "being right."

If a mother cooks a meal she does so because there is an *objective need* for feeding the members of the household. Incidentally, she may also like to cook. If so, she may cook even if there is no pressing need for a meal, just for the pleasure of exercising the fond function. The cooking is then done from a *subjective feeling* rather than an objective need. Presumably, every act has this double motivation. If, as a physician, I treat a patient, I satisfy an objective need for practicing my profession but also a subjective feeling of doing something worth accomplishing. The feeling which I speak of may be either painful or pleasurable. For the present, I shall consider those situations only in which action is accompanied by a sense of pleasure exclusively or predominantly.

Temperamental Behavior Feeds on Two
Pleasurable Subjective Feelings

In temperamental behavior, there can hardly be an objective need for the tantrum. Here, everything is subjective feeling. In releasing a temper outburst, you give off steam and experience the pleasurable sense of relief. After you have given free rein to your temper the clear *insight* into the rashness and rudeness of your action prompts you to hunt for an excuse and to rationalize your conduct on the grounds of your being right. To the pleasure of having gained relief from tension is added the further pleasure of "being right." In this manner, each temperamental act feeds on two pleasurable subjective feelings. How can you ever expect to give up a habit voluntarily if it attracts you with the almost irresistible lure of one pleasure topping the other?

I told you that Edna and George were what you would call "nice people." If you scan the list of your friends you will observe that most persons with an explosive temper belong to the class of "nice people." This seems to be a contradiction. What you expect of "nice people" is precisely that they keep a vigilant eye on their behavior and correct it whenever their insight tells them that their action offends against a standard. The temperamental person, I said, has insight into the inexcusable nature of his explosions. If he belongs to the class of "nice people," why does the insight fail to curb his temper? The answer ought to be plain: the man with a temper has insight into the ugliness of his conduct but the double pleasure of securing relief from tension and adding the sense of "being right" blocks his customary intention to be "nice." The double premium of pleasure placed on temper behavior prevents insight from asserting itself. Indeed, the temperamental person is vitally interested in silencing the voice of insight. Should he heed it, it would deprive him of the coveted relief from tension and of the stimulating sense of being right. Temperament is the enemy of insight. In order to blot it out it invents the excuse of "being right." Again I remind you of my statement that the "sense of being wrong" leads to the "claim to be right." I shall now add that the insight into being wrong calls imperatively for the claim to be right.

Business Is Governed by Impersonal Rights, Family Relations by Personal Sentiments

"Rights" is a term borrowed from the business field of competition and domination and ought to have no place in the home which is the domain of service and cooperation. It would be absurd to say that a baby is given the bottle because it is "by right" entitled to it. All the mother has in mind while feeding the baby is its needs for the milk, or her own needs for tending her offspring. Whether the food is merited, deserved, or earned is, of course, not considered. If the tot cries through the night the parents, although deprived of their comfort, do not think of questioning the baby's right to cause the disturbance. The same holds true of other relationships between parents and children. A father provides for needs and comforts, not because the children have vested rights but because of affection, interest, love, pride, and other sentiments which have nothing or little to do with consideration of rights.

In business, "rights" reign supreme. A laborer receives just as much compensation for his work as he has a right to demand. Business transactions are, as a rule, drawn up in the form of contracts. If one of the contracting parties fails to live up to his obligations he forfeits his contractual rights. In the family no rights are forfeited because of default. If a wayward son absconds with the father's money, in nine cases out of ten he is certain of indulgence and forgiveness. Business activities are governed by impersonal rights, family relations by highly personal sentiments.

However, it is well known that enlightened self-interest taught business men to use tact and courtesy in dealing with employees. Moreover, if a clerk is discharged, the average employer has full insight into the fact that hardship is inflicted and misery created. He is not likely to obscure or block the insight by insisting that he is right and the employee wrong. He does not moralize or rationalize but advances the realistic reason that business necessities call for economy and retrenchment.

Mother's Determination to Be Right Causes Relapse of Recovered Daughter

Agnes, a girl of 22, recovered and was sent home. During the last weeks of hospital residence she had enjoyed the ordinary privileges of a recovering patient. She was permitted to take walks on the hospital grounds and to go on the street without supervision. When Agnes arrived in the parents' home the mother lost no time taking matters in hand and superintending every step of her daughter. The "darling" had to take it easy, to get her proper rest, and to leave everything to the care of the solicitous mother. When the patient protested that she felt relaxed and had not the slightest trace of fatigue the mother countered with the subtle remark, "Are we going to have these arguments again? You ought to know by now that it was the arguments that broke your health." The daughter meekly suggested, "I didn't have arguments in the hospital," whereupon the mother terminated the discussion by the peremptory statement, "I guess I can't help it if you don't listen. But you'll have to blame yourself if something happens again." All protests were in vain and Agnes had to lie on the couch, provoked, outraged, and—not at all resting.

In the afternoon the patient wished to telephone a friend. The mother objected. "Take your time. What's the rush? Why are you so restless?" The minutest details of daily routine were blocked and interfered with as if the mother dealt with a baby that "got into everything." When Agnes spent more time in the bathroom than the mother thought necessary there was a knock at the door and an anxious inquiry, "Don't you feel well, dear?" At meal times the injunctions, warnings, and prohibitions followed one another with rapid fire speed. "Why don't you start? . . . You better take this tender piece, this one will not agree with you . . . one potato is enough; you better take more cauliflower . . . " After three days of continuous harassment of this kind the daughter began to assert herself. The mother's insistence provoked resentment; resentment turned into spite. Finally the very voice of the mother was a source of irritation. The atmosphere was charged with mutual antagonism. In the evening of the eighth day the mother insisted again on the daughter's taking a rest. There was a sudden flare-up and violent argument. Agnes felt a choking sensation, became frantic with rage and flung herself at the mother ready to strike her. The father pulled the two apart but was unable to control the hysterical outburst. The daughter went on raving, sobbing, and yelling. In the end it was decided to return her to the hospital. When the mother gave to the physician her account of the events preceding the readmission she punctuated her narrative with the ever-recurring inquiry, "Don't you think I was right? . . . Wasn't that the right thing to do? . . . Wouldn't it have been wrong on my part to let her do as she pleased?" Again, the sense of being wrong leading to the incessant claim to be right. And at the end of the path to righteousness lies the helpless victim that recovered her mental health only to have it sacrificed to the mother's determination to be right.

Insight Is Dimmest If Domination Hides
Behind Disguise of Service

Agnes' mother also belonged in the class of "nice people." She was a conscientious mother,, a loyal wife, a generous friend. The tragedy was that she "stood on her rights," and was ready to defend them though it might mean a fight to the finish. Even after the daughter had plunged back into the darkness of mental derangement the question uppermost in the mother's mind was whether or not she had acted right. Instead of adjusting to the daughter's *objective needs* for a modicum of privacy and self-management she acted on her own *subjective urge* to enforce maternal supervision. On the face of it she was anxious and concerned about Agnes' welfare and seemed actuated by a spirit of service. In one of my next lectures I shall dwell at length on this deadly bane of domestic life: domination disguised in the cloak of service. For the present, I shall give you in conclusion the following distinction, from the viewpoint of insight, between the three different patterns of domination which I described. First, there was the employer who discharged a worker. He exercised domination with good insight into the oppressive nature of his act. The insight was unobscured by pretense or excuse. Second, the husband who ignored or tyrannized over his wife. He had adequate insight into the objectionable and domineering quality of his behavior but the insight was clouded and blocked by his claim to be right. Third, Agnes' mother who harassed her daughter to the point of distraction. Her domineering attitude was so thoroughly overlaid with a deceptive appearance of service that insight, if at all operative, was at its dimmest. The dimming was successfully effected by the cloak of service that was spread over the acts of domination. It will be easy for you relatives to realize that this type of behavior which uses service as disguise for domination is the most dangerous for the peace and health of the returned patient.

It is hardly necessary to add a comment to Lecture 7. The theme is in direct succession to the topic discussed in the preceding chapters and integrates well with the total pattern. In the following chapters the subjects of temper control and will training will be resumed in their various implications with the theme merely continued and the pattern preserved. Comments will be added only when called for by special considerations.

LECTURE 8

THE INFANTILE ORIGIN OF TEMPER

Temperamental people are in the habit of explaining their explosions and violent reactions by the excuse that they "can't help it," that they "must" and "have to" explode because their temper is their "nature." In other words, they not only disclaim responsibility but slander nature to boot. Somewhere in the recesses of their thought is the vague idea that their temperamental behavior is the result of inborn instincts which were inherited from their forbears. If this were true the attempt to change temper would be doomed. How can one hope to effect a radical change in a trend that is inborn, natural, instinctual and hereditary?

At the risk of being intolerably monotonous and repetitious I shall recite the well-known fact that temperamental persons, as a rule, display their tempers solely or mainly with the members of their immediate family and with their employees. In the company of strangers and friends, and particularly in the presence of "important" people, like superiors, hosts and hostesses, their nature is pleasingly tamed, their instinct neatly controlled and their heredity conveniently forgotten. Most of it is clearly not inborn but acquired.

Whatever else may be the meaning of temperamental behavior one thing is plain: underlying it is emotion. There is emotion without temper but there is no temper without emotion. I do not presume to know what is the nature of emotion. I shall have to tell you something about its meaning and function, however, regardless of whether my account will be sufficiently pertinent or complete.

Emotions Are Either Elemental or Incidental

Some emotions arise spontaneously without anything in the environment apparently being responsible for their emergence. For some unknown reason a person is suddenly thrown into a fit of moroseness or sadness; another person, for equally unknown reasons, suddenly experiences a wave of joy and well being. No explanation can be given for the unexpected shift in feelings. The thing simply happens and cannot be accounted for on the basis of present circumstances or preceding events. Emotions of this kind assail and overwhelm the individual with the abruptness of a change in the elements (cloudburst, snowstorm). They may therefore be called *elemental emotions*. On the other hand, there are emotions which are directly traceable to external events. A familiar example is the reaction of the inexperienced mother who witnesses a tantrum thrown by her little son. There is a sudden stoppage of breathing—an innocent breath-holding spell. No special manipulation is required to terminate the youngster's antics. If left to himself the spell will spend itself and normal breathing will be quickly resumed; or, a few drops of cold water will revive respiration with the promptness of magic. But to the mother it looks like dreadful danger and impending disaster. Her frightened screams make the neighbor hurry to the scene who, more experienced, restores the child's breathing with a jet of cold water. After that, the mother who had been mortally alarmed but a few seconds ago instantly dismisses the fear and is overjoyed with happiness. In an instance of this sort, one environmental event, the breath-holding of the child, produced fear, and another environmental event, the restoration of breathing, caused the fear to change to joy. The rise and fall of the emotions was here incidental to happenings in the environment and the reactions were, therefore, due to *incidental emotions*. That incidental emotions can hardly be unchangeable may safely be assumed. If a gunman points a loaded pistol at my head, the danger is realistic and my emotion called-for and justified by the gravity of the incident. However, if a man is afraid of riding in an elevator there is no realistic danger in the incident and the resulting emotion is unjustified and uncalled-for. The ride is merely thought to be dangerous and the elevator merely stands for or symbolizes the idea of danger. What the man fears is a symbolic rather than realistic danger.

Realistic Dangers Are Frequently Ignored

The average man is surprisingly indifferent to realistic dangers. Otherwise, how is it possible that men are ready to risk their lives daily and hourly for the sheer pleasure of racing their automobiles? In a city of moderate size death and crippledom threaten at every corner but hardly anybody troubles to take the necessary precaution. Think of the astounding equanimity with which the average person engages in hazardous occupations and in daring sports activities, and you will readily agree that realistic dangers are generally ignored or even flouted.

There are realistic dangers which are inevitably attended by violent fears. But even their frightening effect is soon neutralized by that miraculous capacity of the average human being which we call adjustment. If a child is seriously ill the mother is certainly alarmed, perhaps to the point of distraction. However, if the child dies it usually takes a few months before the parents are either sensibly resigned to the misfortune or comforted by the prospect of having or adopting another child. I could remind you of the well-known instances of disaster which we all witnessed during the early stages of the economic depression which burst upon us in 1929. Millions of persons went bankrupt and lost their positions and life savings, but most of them rearranged their affairs and were soon prepared to face the wreckage with sober resignation. You may draw the conclusion that realistic dangers are either generally ignored or easily adjusted to. You may draw the further inference that dangers which defy ready adjustment and give rise to sustained or chronic fears are suspect of being symbolic in nature.

I have frequently spoken to you of the adverse effect which the fear of being wrong exercises on domestic life. This fear is undoubtedly sustained and chronic, lasting a lifetime with most individuals. It defies adjustment with stubborn tenacity, and few are those who have learned to face it with composure and fewer yet those who know how to ignore it. This alone is sufficient to mark it off as the fear of a symbolic danger. It will now be my task to explain to you what precisely is meant by the terms "symbol" and "symbolic danger."

Realism Deals With Objective Measurment, Symbolism With Subjective Feelings

A woman dies. The physician, weary after a strenuous night's vigil, departs, leaving the afflicted husband and children to their grief and sorrow. Gradually, a group of sympathetic friends and neighbors foregather in the dimly lit room and are soon joined by relatives summoned from more distant sections. Finally, the clergyman arrives, and in the end the undertaker puts in his sombre appearance. To all of them the deceased woman meant or symbolized something. She was a wife, mother, sister, aunt, friend, neighbor, patient and parishioner. Even to the undertaker, for all his official imperturbability, she most likely meant or stood for or symbolized suffering mankind.

Then comes stark realism: the death certificate must be made out and signed by the attending physician. This document lists the dead body as belonging to one Jane Jones, 58 years of age, 5 feet 7 inches tall, having been a resident of Chicago, Cook County. It records, with cool and impersonal indifference, that the deceased had been ill from September 11 to October 27, 1939 and that she expired at 8:34 A.M. in consequence of a myocardial degeneration, etc., etc.

The certificate spoke of height and age, of the time of death and the duration of the diseaase. It added a few remarks of a geographical nature (address and place of residence) and finally stated the name of the illness which terminated life. All of it was impersonal, unfeeling and mathematical. Certainly, the fact that the patient measured several feet and inches, had lived a certain number of years and resided in a certain locality is no index to what the deceased meant or stood for or symbolized to the mourners. To them she symbolized motherhood and wifehood, humanity and friendship, loyalty and kindness. The children adored her, the husband loved her, the more distant relatives, friends and neighbors valued her qualities and treasured the memories of common joys and sufferings. You see the difference; realism deals with what can be *objectively measured,* symbolism with what must be *personally felt.* *

Symbolism, Emotions and Self-Valuation Are Closely Interrelated

To an adult person, an apple will hardly ever stand for or symbolize a personal feeling. Instead, it will be objectively measured as to whether it is red or yellow, sweet or sour, ripe or green, big or small, expensive or cheap. To a child, on the other hand, an apple may symbolize something that arouses keen personal feelings. For some reason he tries to take hold of it but discovers painfully that he is unable to reach it. He struggles, climbs laboriously on the chair, tugs at the tablecloth and if finally successful in grabbing it utters a triumphnt yell. To secure the apple is to him a symbol of *strength and success.* On the other hand, if he fails

---

*Impersonal symbols, like mathematical signs, trade emblems, road markers, etc., are here neglected as having no bearing on personal adjustment.

in his effort there will be a wail or cry of discomfiture. He will resent his inability to obtain the desired object and sense it a symbol of *weakness and failure*. The success aroused in him the emotions of joy, happiness and delight, the failure those of anger, grief and resentment. In either case, the event was not merely objectively described and measured but subjectively valued. The boy was proud of his attainment or unhappy over the lack of it. His success enhanced the value of his ego, his failure reduced that value. Both gave rise to his primitive code of *self-valuation*. You see here the intimate interrelation between emotion, symbol and valuation.

It has been said that the child discovers the symbolism of his self-value at an early stage of his development. This is supposed to happen when one day, in a moment of immature self-observation, he is struck by the fact that when he wants to move his arm he can do so "at will." At this moment, the theory continues, he becomes aware of his ability and power, in other words, his self-value. Enjoying the movement which discloses his power he repeats the act and, overwhelmed with the exhilarating evidence of his self-value, keeps repeating the performance in endless sequences. Be this as it may, the fact is that children are fond of repeating their performances in uncounted series. Moreover, at a later age, they frequently accompany their repetitious manipulations with the self-confident comment, "Look what I do." At this stage it is a common observation that when a child is handed a cookie he may reply, "Put it back. I want to take it myself." Obviously, the child cherishes and values his power of *self-management and self-direction*.

The Infantile Table of Valuation Leads to Primitive Form of Domination

Gradually the infantile table of valuation grows and extends its ever increasing store of symbolilisms. As the months and years pass the child is no longer content with managing and directing his own self, he aspires to the direction of others. He sees an object on the table and could easily fetch it but delights in asking daddy to get it for him. Mother asks him to put on his shoes but he suggests, "You put them on for me." The maid prepares to dress him as she always does. But the youngster wants to be dressed by daddy. He rejoices in ordering his parents about, insists on being lifted and swung and otherwise played with. He makes the mother tell him stories and read to him, all of it in a peremptory, dictatorial manner. If he has already reached the state of mastery of language he reels off question after question, some of them revealing a genuine curiosity and interest, most of them, however, undoubtedly intended to make others speak and return answers. The others must do what he wants them to do. He manages and directs their activities. The valuational symbolism for *primitive leadership* has been created and leadership is conceived by the tot as meaning reckless use of power.

On goes the process of development. New symbols are formed and the childish table of valuation enlarged. After the child has learned to rejoice in the delights of self-management and leadership he is currently thwarted in the exercise of both values. He is just busy playing with his toys when mother calls him to the bathroom. He ignores the call and continues toying with his blocks. Mother calls again, and he still pays no attention. Finally he is brusquely grabbed by the arm and dragged away from his favorite activity. The experience is decidedly one that he does not cherish or value. His primitive temper is aroused; he resents the interference, revolts against mother's effort to manage him and offers opposition and resistance. Mother may be reasonably strict but frequently she weakens and gives in. Then the child experiences the thrill of triumph. In the course of time he has numerous occasions to enjoy the delight of forcing his will on the others, of resisting them, of denying their requests. The symbols of conquest, of victory and triumph are formed. The child has now created the valuational symbolism of *primitive domination*.

The Child as Enemy of the "Conditional Standard"

After the child develops domination as the leading feature of his primitive table of valuation his mind is increasingly focused on antagonism, opposition and resistance. His main aim is now to score victories and to subdue others. People and things assume a symbolic meaning. Heretofore, mother was a person with realistic functions; she gave help when he was in distress, provided entertainments when he desired them, put him to sleep when he was tired and fed him when he was hungry. Now she is reduced to the status of an empty figure in a strange world in which the son hunts for symbolic values. In this weird world of his the chief values attach to the symbol of victory. A prospective victor must have somebody to vanquish, to humble, to provoke and to irritate. Mother is assigned this role of the punching bag and whipping boy. As such she plays the symbolic part of a victim and the boy that of a victor. Symbolism becomes now the keynote of existence. Potatoes are no longer realistic food; they are merely a welcome opportunity to refuse to eat them. Mother will then humble herself and implore him to take "a tiny spoonful at least" and he will revel in the sight of a helpless victim of his domination. Before long he notices that when he is recalcitrant and resistive father and mother beg him to be nice and to act like a good boy. In some vague form he senses the distinction between good people and bad people and dimly realizes that objectionable manners are the surest means of antagonizing the parents and of scoring victories over them. He now embarks on a systematic campaign to initiate a naughty course of behavior. Mother cautions him not to climb on the window sill, and he does it with gusto. She wants him to be clean "like a good boy"; so he contrives to soil his clothes whenever he I has an opportunity. He has perhaps never heard the word "standard of behavior" but knows how to offend it with uncanny mastery. His conduct degenerates into a riot against the standard of good manners. As his rebellious course continues he becomes a sworn enemy of everything regulated by the so-called "conditional standard."

Infantile Conflicts Result in Disguise of Domination Behind Pretense of Service

Occasionally the meek mother refuses to do his bidding. Then he resorts to screaming, whining and nagging. He soon notices that such conduct is particularly likely to antagonize and provoke mother. The screaming, whining and nagging are now practiced routinely. Somewhere he picks up a word of profanity. Mother is horrified and pleads with him not to use: it. Henceforth he rejoices in repeating the few expletives he happens to know. In due course he develops a talent for choosing that type of behavior that is certain to scandalize the parents. Their horror is then skillfully utilized to make them yield to his wishes. You say he has an ugly temper, but essentially he is nothing but a radical devotee of his childhood philosophy which drives him to accumulate an imposing record of symbolic victories over helpless victims. It is this philosophy that impels him to develop an unruly temper and to adopt the manners of a ruthless bully.

At six he enters school. There he tries his bullying manner with the other children but is severely handled. In repeated encounters of this kind he learns that temperamental behavior is badly misplaced in the new environment. Forced by dire necessity he mends his ways. He practices a pleasing deportment and gradually acquires the habits of courtesy and consideration. A cooperative spirit is substituted for the bullying propensity. In his contact with outsiders his behavior becomes impeccable and carefully adjusted to the requirements of the conditional standard. But this change takes place on the outside only. At home he still indulges his craving for ruthless domination. However, his approach is modified. He has been exposed to the mellowing influence of religious education, has imbibed the philosophy of service and cooperation taught him by his teachers and has passed through the school of self-discipline and team work imposed on him by group games with classmates. He acquires a socially oriented table of valuation and its effect carries over into the home atmospheere. When he now loses his temper and releases a tantrum he is oppressed by a sense of shame and has a distressing insight into the obnoxiousness of his misbehavior. His present group values of service and his pristine infantile values of domination clash and throw him into a violent inner conflict. That conflict must be solved and the solution is found in a gradually maturing system of *disguising domination behind the pretense of service.*

Misbehavior Is Excused on the Flimsy Pretense of Duty and Obligation

His mother is busy tending the baby and requests him to make some purchases at the nearby grocery store. In his pre-school years he was in the habit of offering undisguised refusal on such occasions. Or, he might pretend not to hear even if the request was repeated several times. Or, he stalled and called back, "I have to go to the bathroom" and then spent endless time on the toilet seat doing nothing more urgent than playing with the faucet or tearing up the paper. This was ill-concealed obstruction and well-nigh frank disobedience. Such candid display of antagonism would now shock his new set of values and throw him into the throes of torturing compunctions. This must be avoided. He must devise a scheme which will permit him to give his domination the appearance of service. According to his new set of values it is his duty to obey mother. But there are other duties, for instance, the duty to do his home work. If the two duties cannot be performed at the same time one of them must be neglected in favor of the other. And so he adopts an ingenious method of blocking, repelling and resisting the parents' wishes and pleas on the excuse that other duties and obligations have a prior call. He claims to be busy with home work if asked to do an errand, to have to prepare a report for the next Boy Scouts' meeting when approached with some other request. The procedure permits him to be discourteous and uncooperative without causing a stir in his tender conscience.

The new formula works. It conceals conveniently his domineering temper behind the smoke screen of a dutiful disposition. He can now be impatient, demanding, and even abusive and charge it all to necessity, obligation and moral command. After arising he dawdles in the bathroom and when reprimanded for delaying the older sister's morning toilet he counters with the snappy reply, "I have to be clean at school, haven't I?" He shares his room with a younger brother and manages to disturb his activities or his sleep with some "must" or "have to" or "can I help it if . . . ?" Shortly after the brother has fallen asleep he reminds himself that he forgot to finish some chapter of required reading. He then jumps out of bed with studied noise, turns on all the lights and floods the room with a blazing brightness. His rummaging among books and papers is designedly loud, his steps on the floor unnecessarily heavy and his incessant pulling of drawers and moving of chairs annoyingly disturbing. When the brother remonstrates the reply is, "Can I help it if the teacher gives me too much work?" His ancient craving for scoring symbolic victories and beholding symbolic victims can now be easily satisfied on the flimsy pretense of a "must" or "have to."

The new method of screening temperamental rudeness behind the pretense of moral compulsion is at first limited to the defense of his own wrongdoing; gradually, however, its field of application is extended to include savage attacks on the wrongfulness of others. He misses his fountain pen and turns with righteous fury against mother, "Can't you be more careful? Must you always muss up my desk?" In the morning, he does not find the school book. This gives him the desired opportunity to let loose. "Where is my American History?" he keeps yelling through the house. "I had it on my dresser. Didn't I tell you to leave my things alone? Can't I ever have order in my room?" He is critical, argumentative and insulting, always basing his assaults on pious consideration for duty and responsibility.

Introspection and Insight Disturb Workings of New Strategy

The one thing that is in the way of his fully enjoying his new strategy is his normal capacity for introspection. As is the habit with the average individual, he scrutinizes the value off his actions and finds them wanting. In spite of his moral alibis he cannot avoid the realization that his conduct is rude. The fact that his mother suffers and that the peace of the home is disturbed by his pugnaciousness is so glaring that he cannot possibly ignore it. For all his bravado he is unable to escape a burning sense of guilt. The problem of right and wrong becomes an acute issue. He solves it in the manner which I outlined when I discussed the subject of conflict and insight. The sense of being wrong leads him to the incessant claim to be right. His incessant claims to be right give him a new impetus to initiate fights and to enjoy the sight of victims.

At 25 he marries and acts the role of the "problem adult." However, his wife is not his mother and what the latter condoned the former is determined not to tolerate. Gradually the marital situation degenerates into what I described as the "temperamental deadlock." In the end he is a failure from the viewpoint of adjustment. What wrecked his adjustive career was the system of disguising domination behind the cloak of service. In one of my forthcoming lectures I shall endeavor to show you that the best means of forestalling this adjustment-wrecking system is to cultivate insight to the point of making it impossible for individuals to practice this monstrous device of self-deception. But in order to dispel self-deception efficiently the current misconception that temper is unchangeable must be exploded. Keep in mind that the emotions which form the basis of temper are not elemental but incidental. Keep also in mind that temperamental persons fight for infantile symbols rather than adult realities. Incidental emotions can be controlled and infantile symbols can be shed by means of proper insight. The precise method of how this can be effected I shall attempt to demonstrate in the near future.

LECTURE 9

SYMBOLS AND THEIR INTERPRETATIONS

In my last few lectures I described the manner in which temper arises from symbolisms developed in childhood. I demonstrated that children form infantile symbols of triumph and victory which provide the background for future temperamental dispositions. The object of the subsequent lectures is to continue with the analysis of temper in order to teach you how to dispose of infantile symbolisms for the purpose of paving the way for adult realistic conduct.

Objects and Actions Have Both
Realistic and Symbolic Meanings

Every object which you possess, every act that you perform, every sentence that you speak has both a realistic and symbolic meaning. When you buy a coat you think that you are guided by realistic considerations for durability, monetary value and protection against rain and cold. No doubt you are. But a good part of your money is unquestionably spent with an eye to your social status. Color, style and pattern are so chosen that they represent or symbolize your relative importance in your social group. Or, you own a house and it serves the realistic function of a shelter, but it may also represent or symbolize such unrealistic qualities as community opinion, personal dignity and family tradition. To quote another example: your automobile is, realistically enough, a means of transportation. But will you deny that it also symbolizes your financial capacity? Morever, if you race along the road, you may actually pursue the realistic purpose of saving time. But you will admit that frequently you speed and pass other vehicles and beat the street car to the corner without being hard pressed for time. Is it realistic and sensible to risk your life for the pleasure of overtaking another driver, or for the glory of competing with street cars? Let me tell you that what secures pleasure in such instances is something purely symbolic: when you pass a driver you score a symbolic victory over another person; you enter into symbolic competition with the street car when you shoot ahead of it and you conquer—symbolically—space and time when you can pile up a record of—say—two hundred miles in three or four hours. These examples will demonstrate that even the most common objects and acts have a considerable symbolic content side by side with their realistic meaning.

If the pattern and style of your coat fittingly symbolize your social importance you like them and may even be proud of them. You certainly adore your home if you feel it represents symbolically beauty, dignity and family tradition. And that you may grow enthusiastic over the superior performance of your car is clearly evidenced by the fact that you are ready to boast of its "marvelous pickup" at the least provocation. You see, if an object of your possession symbolizes power of any kind yon enjoy it, feel proud of it, speak of it in enthusiastic terms and boast of its excellence. What I am driving at here is that symbols evoke *sentiments*.

I spoke of symbols residing in objects and mentioned coats, houses and automobiles as symbolizing power. I could have selected any arbitrary assortment of things and events, and it would have been easy to prove that all of them have both a realistic and symbolic component. The cigar which you smoke has the realistic function of providing stimulation but also the symbolic connotation that it is relatively expensive and that you can afford the price. You may refrain from using a less expensive brand for the sole reason that it might not be the fitting symbol for your social status. Your tie and your gloves, your brief-case and wrist watch belong in the same category. They have a symbolic representation side by side with their realistic function and you like them and may even be proud of them as expressing symbolically your social or economic power.

A Mother Is Not Judged by Realistic Criteria

The most important symbols are those representing persons. Here is a woman, 48 years of age, five feet eight inches tall, her hair grayish, her eyes blue, her walk steady but cautious. I could add a description of the color and texture of her skin, of the shape of her nose, of the regularity or irregularity of her features, of the proportional size of trunk and limbs, and what I would furnish would be a factual account of her realistic appearance. But if I know that the woman is your mother my description is trite, banal and meaningless. You simply do not judge your mother by realistic criteria. Let her have a hunchback, and her symbolic value to you will not diminish one iota. Let her waste away and shrivel to ugly proportions; she will still be adored and loved by you as the symbol of motherhood, devotion, kindness and self-effacement. Even after death wipes out her realistic existence altogether she is still your cherished symbol of motherhood which you worship in loving remembrance.

What I said of the mother applies with equal or similar force to wife, daughter, son, father, indeed, to all persons who are close to you, either as relatives and friends, or as colleagues, partners and classmates. The closer they stand to your heart the stronger counts their symbolic value, the less significant is their realistic existence.

The Physical "Self" Is Symbolically Distinct From the Social "Self"

Nobody is perhaps inclined to think of himself in terms of symbolism. On the contrary, everybody seems to pride himself on being a realist. Yet, what is called the "self" is little more than an aggregate of symbols. However, the term "self" admits an ambiguity of interpretations, and in order to avoid confusion it will be advisable to define in as simple words as possible what precisely is meant by it.

In the morning, when you arise you throw your robe around your "self," then you shave and wash your "self." Judging from your smile and whistle, it is fair to assume that while performing all these successive acts you enjoy your "self." After you finish washing and shaving you give your "self" the benefit of a refreshing shower. Finally, you terminate the morning toilet and remove your "self" to the dining room. There you treat your "self" to fruit, eggs, ham, toast, and coffee. Suddenly you throw a glance at the clock and notice to your dismay that today you will again be late at the office. It is a common occurrence that you can't get your "self" to be on time for your work and your inability to discipline your "self" sufficiently to cease dawdling has always been a "self" humiliating experience to you. You know that nobody is to blame but your "self." Indeed, you are mortified by the fact that you do not have your "self" under sufficient control. In the past you made repeated efforts to overcome this handicap which was anything but a credit to your "self" but no matter how often you told your "self" that things had to change, you seemed to lack sufficient "self" mastery to remedy the situation. In the end, you decided that all you could do was to resign your "self" to the unfortunate situation and to let things take their course.

It will not be difficult for you to realize that the "self" which is washed, shaved, and removed to the dining room and there treated to a meal is significantly distinct from the "self" which is blamed for or credited with some act and finally feels humiliated and becomes resigned to the handicap of a situation. The one is the physical, the other the social "self." Using less familiar but more correct terms, one might call the one the physiological, the other the sociological "self." However, for reasons of simplicity. I shall use the words "physical" and "social."

Slurs to Social "Self" Arouse Tempers

The average adult person is hardly ever sufficiently naive or inane to take credit for the number or size of the eggs which he is capable of consuming; nor is he likely to boast of the artistry of wielding the razor or dressing a sandwich. These manipulations may disclose skill and dexterity but they do not represent or symbolize the value of the "self." At best they could only be symbolic of the accomplishments of the physical "self," and adult individuals are not in the habit of exalting the status of their physical "selves." What they are fond of emphasizing is the excellence of their social "self." This they conceive of, paradoxically enough, as representing or symbolizing their individual worth. In the average person's mind the physical "self" represents nothing but realistic functions while the social "self" is thought of as the jealously guarded repository of qualities which are the symbolic expressions of his personal value.

You may value and cherish the symbolism represented by your coat, automobile, and house. These values will hardly be challenged by anybody. The occasions will be rare when your coat will be insulted, your car slighted or your house ridiculed. And if you love your mother, wife, and daughter, hardly anybody will ever stand in the way of your tender sentiments for these exalted symbols of your inner life. But if you develop the symbolisms of your important, weighty and prominent social "self" the occasions for real or imagined slurs, piques and affronts will be innumerable. A contemptuous shrug on the part of the man you speak to, a quizzical raise of the eyebrow in the countenance of your neighbor with whom you chat a critical intonation in the question asked by your employer, friend, wife or brother will be felt, on a thousand occasions, as a severe challenge to the value of your social self, as an indictment of your moral, esthetic or intellectual integrity. A challenge of this kind is almost certain to cut you to the quick and to provoke your temper. You see here again the close interrelation between symbolism, self-valuation and temper.

The Symbolic Meaning of Social Contacts Is Subject to Interpretation

If two men meet at a party they establish both physical and social contacts. Obviously, the physical contact of sitting face to face or side by side is of no significance under the circumstances. What counts is their social contact. That contact is effected through speech and action. The two may chat, or the one man may offer a cigaret to the other, or both may raise their glasses and drink to one another's health. Whatever they do has the symbolic meaning of being officially polite or sincerely amicable or shrewdly calculating or may be representative of any number of symbolic attitudes. Suppose the one man is an elderly leader of the community, the other a young man who has not yet made his mark, either socially or economically. Then the older man's toast to the health of his younger companion may mean or represent or symbolize a desire to be condescending, and to display a democratic sense of benevolence. If the younger man, encouraged by his partner's friendly demeanor, deems the occasion propitious for clumsy familiarity his behavior may be conceived of as meaning or symbolizing boldness or insolence. In either case, the symbolic meaning of the acts and words are subject to interpretation, correct or incorrect. The point I wish to emphasize here is that symbols must always be *interpreted*.

Temper is usually the result of *misinterpretation of symbols*. Your son, improved but not yet recovered, has just returned from the hospital for a brief week-end visit. After his arrival, you address the innocent question to him, "Why don't you take off your coat and make yourself comfortable?" This plain sentence which, in the main, spoke of such realistic subjects as a coat to be removed and of comfort to be secured, offers a wealth of opportunities for symbolic misinterpretations. Perhaps your remark was meant as a casual suggestion without any significant implication. But to your son, fresh from an environment where everything was strictly regulated and systematized, your statement may symbolize a tendency to superintend his activities, or an urge to criticize his ways, or concern about his state of health. Indeed, it may be taken to represent your fear that he is not visibly improved and still in need of solicitous care. If so, the likelihood is that your plain inquiry will be misinterpreted as unwarranted intrusion or insinuation, and your son's temper will be aroused.

His temper stirring, your son may return the harsh reply, "You don't have to tell me what to do. I am not a kid." You feel provoked by the uncalled-for verbal assault but control your rising anger and calmly suggest, "But John, I didn't mean to insult you. Why are you so sensitive?" Whereupon John, with bitter sarcasm, "Of course, you never mean what you say. But I know your tricks and you can't fool me." And so the passage of words proceeds, your son ablaze with emotion and you anxious to stem the flood of his invective. But the son is intractable and your mild manner powerless to convice him of the innocence of your intentions. Finally, you realize that your words merely serve to fan the flames of his senseless indignation and ignore his ravings. In the end he quiets down and the storm is over.

The Common Man Judges With Common Sense, the Temperamental Person With Special Sensibility

Of course your son is still sick and easily irritated. But

what is at fault is his manner of misinterpreting the symbolic meaning of your approach. When you asked, "Why don't you take off your coat?" the question meant or symbolized to you an expression of legitimate fatherly interest; but to your son it meant or symbolized an intention to "boss" him. Your interpretation of your own intention differed from that of your son's. If a stranger had witnessed the scene he would have shared your opinion and disapproved of your son's misinterpretation. That stranger would have represented the views of the "common man" who gives things their "common interpetation" and acts on "common sense." His final vedict would have been that your interpretation was based on realistic *common sense* while your son's misinterpretation was the result of special personal sensibilities. Mark that temper is a misinterpretation of the symbolic meaning of behavior, based on special personal sensibilities. Such sensibilities go by the name of idiosyncrasies.

When George and Edna reach the impasse of the temperamental deadlock they indulged in orgies of misinterpretations of one another's intentions, expressions and symbolic meanings. At this stage each of them responded to the actions and statements of the marital partner with special personal sensibilities rather than with common sense. On some days George was not in the mood to speak at dinner time and consumed his meal in silence. Edna then passed the ironical remark, "Why, you are certainly lots of fun today. What's the matter? Are you going to start your fussing again?" You see, in her outside contacts, if any of her friends happened to be reticent, Edna used common sense and interpreted the reaction as the impersonal result of fatigue or lack of spontaneity or ordinary preoccupation. The friend's silence did not symbolize hostility or preparation for a fight. But when she was with her husband, anything he might do or say was responded to with special personal sensibility and misinterpreted as meaning or symbolizing unfriendly intentions. George was similarly disposed to be oversensitive and personal and frequently resented Edna's inquiries and requests summarily as attempts to impose on him. When Edna advanced the routine suggestion to go to a show he was likely to misinterpret her approach as lack of consideration and growled back acidly, "Didn't you see the pile of correspondence on my desk? It wouldn't do you any harm to consider my work once in a while. Must you always think of your pleasure?" Common sense was no longer used and the realistic needs for innocent entertainments or for occasional silence grated on special sensibilities; they were misinterpreted as meaning or symbolizing a vicious attempt to interfere with the partner's comfort or to intrude on his or her legitimate pursuits. Domestic peace was wrecked through misinterpretation of common realistic wishes and needs as symbolizing personal and special impositions and animosities.

The Inflated "Self" Experiences Refusals or Denials as Insults and Rebuffs

When George neglected conversation at the table Edna experienced the silence as a slur against her "self." In like manner, when Edna proposed a visit to the theater George experienced the approach as an imposition on his "self." In either case, what was felt as slurred or imposed on was not the physical but the social "self." Cleary, to both of them, their social "selves" represented or symbolized something that was extremely delicate, easily agitated and readily wounded. The "self" of the average, common individual expects in its daily contacts nothing but an average, common measure of deference and consideration. If the average person is denied a request he takes it for granted, as a rule, that the denial was based on some realistic inability or some justified indisposition, dictated by fatigue, lack of time or a well-reasoned dislike of the proposal. The denial does not symbolize to him a personal insult. His "self" is not sufficiently inflated to experience every refusal as affront and every grant as homage to his importance. But suppose you deal with your superior. He does not represent a common person; he symbolizes an exceptional, special individual. If he makes a request it is a business suggestion, hence, something in the nature of a command; if his request is refused the denial is justly experienced as rebellion against his authority. You see, if you are confronted with an important, exceptional and special person you are no longer permitted to use common procedure; instead, you will be wise to show special attention and special consideration. The important person symbolizes a "self" with special sensibilities which are extremely delicate, easily agitated and readily wounded. Requests are experienced as orders, denials as rebuffs.

In the situation of the temperamental deadlock the partners develop the conception of their "selves" as superior, important and brooking no resistance. Edna and George thought of their "selves" as average and common when they were with strangers or friends. But when dealing with one another they experienced their "selves" as specially privileged. To Edna, her own "self" appeared as something superior, entitled to special consideration, and George's "self" as inferior, in duty bound to display deferential behavior and not to balk at her wishes and commands. Since George entertained the same notion about the importance of his own and the insignificance of Edna's "self" there was no common ground for friendly understanding and genial compromise. Marital adjustment ran aground on the reef of special demands and special refusals. Domestic peace was wrecked by the elaboration of a system of symbols which assigned special privileges to the one "self" and denied them to the other.

Mature Knowledge, Combined With
Persistent Practice, Conquers Temper

Recently one of our friends, a diligent visitor of our meetings, made the following comment: "I agree with everything you say; indeed, I know from personal experience that you are right. Moreover, when I listen to your lectures and read in *Lost and Found** your description of Edna and George, I cannot help feeling that you must have repeatedly witnessed the temper outbursts that pass between my wife and me. But doctor, are your explanations going to help me and my wife? I know that we are in a temperamental deadlock and that my impatience and sarcasm are utterly unjust and unreasonable. But no matter how intently I listen to your explanations, I am unable to control my temper. I know I am wrong but that knowledge does not seem to help me."

The author of this comment is a man of fifty with a record of more than twenty years of conjugal temper, according to his own frank avowal. His attendance at Recovery, Inc. meetings dates back six months and his acquaintance with *Lost and Found* is of equally recent origin. Presumably, he began practicing temper control a few months ago and has already discovered that "knowledge does not seem to help him." Obviously, our friend expected quick results to follow hastily acquired knowledge. This seems to be a common misunderstanding among our followers. They apparently entertain the belief that all that is needed to conquer temper is some knowledge—and by no means an excess of it—about its working mechanism.

In reply to this assumption I can merely repeat what I once said to you that "tempers and dispositions can be changed provided the one displaying them (1) acquires

---

*Lost and Found was a bimonthly magazine published by the Recovery Association. It was discontinued September, 1941.

insight and realizes the need for a change of manner, (2) is inspired with the determination to effect the necessary change." (See page 51) I grant that our friend has acquired insight or knowledge, but I doubt whether he is inspired with the requisite determination to practice till the change in temper occurs. You, the relatives of our patients, must keep in mind that what we physicians are able to furnish is knowledge of the problems involved in the subject of domestic temper. The thing that you are required to supply is the determination to practice until control is accomplished. If after a few brief trials you decide that knowledge does not seem to help you, you limited yourself to the one part of our program (the acquisition of insight) but neglected to carry out the other part (the persistent practice based on the newly achieved insight). I am ready to grant our friendly critic one important concession. Thus far I merely endeavored to analyze the ravages inflicted by temper on domestic peace. I also urged you to practice what I tried to teach you. But to date I have not yet made the effort to suggest to you an effective method of practicing temper control. Be certain that relatively detailed instructions on this score will be forthcoming in the future.

LECTURE 10

TEMPER AND RATIONALIZATION

The average salesgirl has an average temper which is sorely tried by the average customer. Yet, as a rule, she exercises control and—keeps her job. If the average husband and wife, father and mother, brother and sister used the simple methods of control employed by the salesgirl, the problem of domestic temper would be solved. The average home would be a scene of peace instead of the customary place of turmoil. What is the salesgirl's method of checking her temper?

*Temper Can Be Effectively Curbed
by a Powerful, Determining Incentive*

First, let me remind you that the salesgirl who is a paragon of sweetness and geniality when provoked by overbearing customers may be impatient, irritable and explosive with members of her own family. Behind the counter she keeps her "self" in check, at the dinner table she lets her "self" go. Obviously, some incentive is operating in the sales room which induces the girl to exercise control, while at home this incentive is missing. You will have no diffculty realizing that the incentive I am speaking of is the determination to keep the job. We conclude that temper can be effectively curbed by a powerful, determining *incentive*. We draw the further inference that domestic discord could be disposed of if powerful incentives for temper control could be established at home.

You can learn something about the workings of a strong incentive if you watch Norma, the salesgirl, waiting on buyers. A lady is standing at the counter, her carriage haughty, her countenance belligerent. Sputteringly, she blusters forth, "How long has a customer to wait in this store till you girls are ready to take an order?" and turning to her neighbor, she continues, in subdued tones but loud enough for Norma to hear, "Of course, all they have in mind is their dates. Honestly, I think it's an outrage." A blush of indigation hovers over Norma's features but is instantly drowned out by a sweet if not wholly convincing smile. "I am sorry, Madam," she pleads ingratiatingly, "I had to take care of this lady. Can I now be of service to you?"

The "Temperamental Cycle" Passes From Insult Over "Emotional Flare-up" to "Explosive Reaction"

In this example the lady's remark was insulting. Norma felt the insult and experienced a momentary flare-up of emotion but checked the impulse before it developed into an explosion. Had the explosion taken place the *temperamental cycle* would have been complete. This cycle begins with the *insult or affront* which is offered by one person and felt by another; it then proceeds to the state of the *emotional flare-up* and ends with the *explosive reaction*. The latter is either motor (actual fight) or verbal (tongue lashing).

In the course of her eight hours' working day Norma is the defenseless target of many affronts and insults. Each of them provokes the emotional flare-up. But none develops into the explosive reaction. Translated into our terminology, this means: whenever Norma deals with customers she manages invariably to leave the temperamental cycle incomplete. An insulting remark strikes her; she flares up but does not explode. You will now understand that what we call temper control is a type of behavior in which the temperamental cycle is left incomplete.

In the evening when Norma reaches her home there are no impudent customers to affront her. Her mother is sweet and soft spoken; her sister and brother are reasonably good natured, considerate and accommodating. You would think that, under the circumstances, Norma has no occasion even to initiate the temperamental cycle. Since nobody insults her why should there be a flare-up? And without a flare-up how could there be an explosion? What you expect is that, at home, Norma should not even experience an incomplete temperamental cycle. Yet it is precisely at home that Norma sets the temperamental cycle going to its ultimate completion. There she misinterprets too many acts and statements as insults, experiences the emotional flare-up and follows it through with the explosive reaction. At home only she permits herself the luxury of the *complete temperamental cycle*.

This is what happens frequently when Norma arrives at her mother's home in the evening. It is seven o'clock. The main dinner course is finished but dessert not yet served. Norma leaves her seat hurriedly, exclaiming, "I can't wait any longer. I have to meet Charles at 7:30." The mother suggests meekly, "I don't undersand why you are in such a hurry. Charles isn't your boss. He will wait a few minutes." Norma's temper rises. "That's my business," she snaps back with a shrill voice, "I will not let anybody interfere with my private affairs." With this she slips into her coat, arranges headgear and makeup and departs, closing the door with a slam.

Norma Practiced the Incomplete Temperamental Cycle
Behind the Counter and Completed the Cycle
at the Dinner Table

Mark the contrast: while serving her customers Norma suffers real insults and humiliations; yet she controls her temper and checks the flare-up before it develops into an explosion. When dealing with her mother there is hardly ever an insult, certainly no indignity and humiliation; yet, temper is released and the flare-up blithely carried over to the stage of the explosion. Why does Norma practice the method of the incomplete temperamental cycle with her customers and not with her mother? Of course, I mentioned that the possible loss of the job acts as a powerful incentive for checking the flare-up. But it would seem that considerations for the peace of the home and the happiness of the mother ought to have considerable strength as incentives, too. Why, then, are they not effective?

Norma is fond of Charles who is a lovable sort of person but easily ruffled and not always in the best of humor. On many occasions he has passed critical remarks that gave a violent jolt to Norma's feelings. Yet, all she experienced was a momentary flare-up; the explosion did not develop. Clearly, the concern about the job is not the only incentive strong enough to curb Norma's temper. The desire to enjoy Charles' company and to retain his friendship has temper controlling power of equal or comparable strength.

What I said of Norma's reaction to Charles is true of other associations. She is frequently irritated by some of her girl friends but seldom loses her temper with them. Occasionally, she is annoyed by a neighbor or by a plain stranger. Here again, her temper flares but does no explode. You see, the consideration for the security of the job, for the permanence of love relations, for friendship, neighborliness and even plain, indifferent contacts are strong incentives for temper control. But domestic peace, if an incentive at all, is utterly lacking in controlling power. What is the reason for this seemingly absurd discrimination?

Business Policy Dictates the Objective Attitude That the "Customer Is Right"

When Norma entered upon her selling career she received a brief course of instruction about business manners and sales policies. Topping the list of rules was the well-known slogan that "the customer is always right." With this slogan in mind, Norma started out on her selling expedition. In the beginning it was difficult to live up to the slogan. Many customers were rude, unreasonable, dictatorial and outright insulting. She was frequently the butt of stinging remarks and biting sarcasm and on such occasions her *subjective disposition* was to strike back and to "stand on her rights." But the fear of losing the job, i.e., the desire for economic security, made her take the *objective attitude* that, after all, the "customer was right." However, there was no danger of economic insecurity at home. There was no "boss" at the dinner table, and to be subjective and emotional there did not mean to incur the danger of being "fired."

At the End of a Tantrum Is Pleasure, at Its Beginning, the Anticipation of Pleasure

If a man gives way to his temper he gains the subjective pleasure of "getting something off his chest" or of "getting even with somebody" or of "telling somebody where to get off." Essentially, these pleasures are due to a sense of having scored a victory over an adversary. You know the keen satisfaction which you experience when you "put somebody in his place" or "tell him what you think of him" or "give him a piece of your mind." On all these occasions you have the soothing sensation of asserting yourself and of displaying strength, determination and virility. You are proud of being "forthright in language," of "shooting straight from the shoulder" and of "calling a spade a spade." The phrases which I quoted are all expressive of the simple fact that you were strong and your opponent weak, that you had the better of the argument and were victorious in the encounter. You gave a good account of yourself and are satisfied with the performance. You will now understand that at the end of a temper tantrum there is always the feeling of pleasure and, at its beginning, the anticipation of pleasure.

This is the crux of the issue of temper: the anticipation of pleasure places a premium on the outburst. To curb temper, then, means to forego a keen pleasure. And the average person is not easily induced to give up pleasure even is it is a pleasure that hurts. Do you realize now why temper control is so difficult to achieve?

Norma, insulted by the customer, experienced a flare-up which had the promise of pleasure. She was now keyed up for the explosion. For a brief moment she revelled in the anticipation of a fight and in the expectation of a victory. However, in the next instant she knew, i.e., had the clear *insight* that to give way to her subjective disposition meant to incur the objective danger of being discharged. It was the insight into the threatening danger which made her curb the anticipated pleasure of retaliation. You see here that temper control is dependent on proper insight into the dangers of temperamental behavior. Norma practiced the requisite insight in her business relations and in the sphere of love, friendship and general social contracts but failed to practice it at home.

The Pleasurable Anticipation Counteracts Insight

Plesaure, more particularly its anticipation, is the enemy of insight. I shall give you an illustrative example. While walking along the street you pass a show window where a tempting display of attractive articles catches your eye. A pair of lovely gloves fascinate you and fire your imagination with the anticipation of the keen pleasure you will derive if you buy them. You fairly itch to make the purchase, but insight raises its voice and warns that the price is excessive and the expense unneccessary. Should you heed the promptings of your insight you would take the *objective attitude* that your finances do not permit splurging and the "spending flare-up" would be checked.

But your anticipation of pleasure is too strong to be dismissed so easily. Your *subjective disposition* to possess the gloves persists with the tenseness of a compelling desire. A conflict is now raging within you between insight and pleasurable anticipation, between the objective attitude and the subjective disposition.

While you waver and hesitate the thought strikes you that, after all, with all due regard for economy, a woman owes something to her appearance. And another happy thought floats into your consciousness: your husband wants you to be well dressed. True, the bills pile up and income is scarce and perhaps it would be wiser to save the money for necessities. But the gloves continue their fascination. Why, you could purchase them and then save on other items. And wasn't Mrs. Jones right when yesterday, at the bridge party, she held forth that a smart woman makes her husband spend money on her? Otherwise, the husband will soon take her for granted and settle down to a dull routine. That last consideration, finally, decides the issue, and the purchase is made.

In Temper Outbursts the Irrational Impulse Is Temporarily Halted by Rational Insight But Finally Sanctioned by Rationalizing Self-Deception

The glove incident is typical and has all the elements of tempermental developments in it. Your vanity was "provoked" by the window display; the impulse to buy "flared-up" and resulted in a subjective disposition to spend money. Up to this point everything was emotional and, therefore, *irrational*. Then came the objective attitude that the spending was unwarranted. This was a *rational* consideration. But it was weak and fleeting and, in the end, gave way to a type of reasoning that was neither irrational nor rational but *rationalizing*. You rationalized that although you were about to do an unwise thing, nevertheless you were *right* in doing it.

It is the process of rationalization that is most apt to cloud insight and block its operation. Reduced to its simplest terms, rationalization is self-deception. You have the irrational desire to invest your meager life savings in speculative stock. Sound rational reflection tells you that you jeopardize the welfare of your family. But you rationalize that only "he who wagers wins" and that the stock market offers the only opportunity for a man of moderate means to send his children to college. Your temperamental inclination to plunge into the stock market is brought to a "flare-up" by an *irrational desire,* is temporarily halted by *rational insight* and finally sanctioned by *rationalizing self-deception.* Rationalization makes "right" what insight declares "wrong" and endorses as socially desirable what insight condemns as socially reprehensible. I said that pleasure is the enemy of insight. I shall qualify this statement by adding that pleasure drugs insight by the simple trick of rationalizing "wrong" into "right" and "antisocial" into "social." After eliminating insight it enables you to practice self-deception.

Frequently, after temperamental spats with her mother, Norma felt miserable. She knew that she caused her mother pain and knew that she could easily avoid the disturbance. Moreover, she was clearly aware of the fact that it was only the members of her family that aroused her temper. She knew that her behavior on the outside was dictated by an objective attitude while conduct at home was the result of a subjective disposition. She knew—and the realization was painful—that on the outside the temperamental cycle was hardly ever permitted to run its course while at home it was completed with distressing regularity. But she saved her conscience by the rationalization that mother was unreasonably solicitous and was "wrong" in her continuous attempts to interfere with the daughter's affairs. And once she had deceived herself into the conviction that mother was "wrong" there was nothing to restrain her temper. If mother was wrong that meant Norma was right, and, being right, she was determined to "stand on her rights." The battle for "rights" was on and raged all along the domestic scene.

Rationalizing Self-Deception Could Be Eliminated
at Home by a Method Similar To That Employed
in Business

Our discussion seems to have established that temper cannot be controlled unless self-deceptive rationalization is avoided. I told you several weeks ago which rationalizations are most fatal to domestic peace. You will remember that I mentioned most prominently the "sense of being wrong" as leading to the temperamental "claim to be right." Once the "claim to be right" is raised habitually at home domestic peace is threatened or even doomed.

On the occasion when, sometime in January, 1940, I resumed the discussion of the "claim to be right" I took pains to emphasize that the concepts of "rights," "insults," "rebuffs" are all symbols which are liable to misinterpretations. I told you at that time that the average person is likely to misinterpret his own "social self" as important, weighty and exceptional, and, in consequence, to insist on his right to special consideration. The battle for rights, then, creates the so-called temperamental tangle.

Business executives are well aware of the tendency of humans to deceive themselves into the belief that their views and acts are right and those of others are wrong. Aware of this unfortunate propensity to "put the other fellow in the wrong" the executive decrees dictatorially that the "customer is always right." With this slogan adopted and enforced there is no room left for self-deceptive rationalization to indulge in symbolic misinterpretations of the customer's intentions, his righteousness and wrongfulness. Ever since business executives have introduced this bar to rationalization the customer has enjoyed immunity from temperamental outbursts of the sales person. I ask: if business was able to devise an effective method of eliminating self-deception, symbolism and rationalization, could not a similar method be made to work in the humanely more important precincts of home life?

The Method of Temper Control Is That of Correct, Objective Interpretation of the "Other Man's" Reaction

A business executive, instructing his sales force about the principle of the "customer being right" might hold forth as follows: suppose you tell the prospective buyer that a given article costs two dollars and he becomes worked up over what he considers an exorbitant charge. You try to pacify him but his anger persists and finally he bursts forth, "That's the limit. I think you are a bunch of cut throats." Suppose his ravings continue and your ears are assailed by such cutting words as "crooks," "cheats," "highway robbers." Under such circumstances it would only be natural for you to interpret the remarks as insults to your integrity. It would also be natural for you to resent the insult and to release a temperamental conterattack. In other words, the manner in which you would interpret, resent and react to the customer's harangue would be in perfect accord with what is called "human nature" and "natural disposition." But no matter how natural may be your interpretation, resentment and temperamental response, in our firm there is no room for "natural dispositions" and "human reactions" if they lead to emotional scenes. What we business people are interested in are sales and returns. These are our *objective aims*. If you have the "natural" tendency to interpret the customer's rudeness as personal insult you will have the *subjective desire* to pounce on him and to repel his attack. This is contrary to our business policy. Our business policy demands that the employee, when dealing with customers, shelve his subjective feelings, trends and desires and have nothing in mind but the objective aim of the firm. As employees of our concern you must always practice and cultivate the *objective attitude* and must not permit yourself to give way to your *subjective disposition*. In order to accomplish this you must realize that your "natural" temperamental reaction has three distinct states: (1) you *interpret* the customer's approach as personal insult, (2) you *resent* the insult, (3) your resentment or anger incite your temper to *react*. If you want to avoid the temperamental reaction you must do away with resentment. And in order to eliminate resentment you must not interpret the customer's behavior as a personal insult. Your temper cannot be held down unless you train yourself to avoid interpretation in terms of personal insults.

It was some such instruction which Norma received when she was hired by her firm. After the preliminary coaching she immediately began "training" herself to refrain from interpreting the words and actions of customers in terms of personal insult. She cultivated the impersonal, objective attitude and, as a result, kept her job. But at home it was difficult to be impersonal and objective. There she did not refrain from interpreting her mother's words and reactions in terms of personal insults. There her "natural disposition" and "human reaction" led to personal interpretation, strong resentment and explosive reactions. Why was it impossible for Norma to practice the method of "non-interpretation" at home? The answer to this question I shall try to give in one of our coming lectures. For the present, I shall content myself with emphasizing that the method of temper control is essentially a method of correct, objective interpretation of the "other man's" reactions.

In Lecture 10 a practical example is introduced of the average salesperson who is compelled to control temper and does so successfully. It is good practice in group instruction to choose such a striking example as the salesgirl and to make it the subject of successive discussions As is evident from the preceding lectures, the author favors the method of grouping his explanations and illustrations around concrete persons. George and Edna served well as examples of the "temperamental deadlock" which is apt to develop in the marital relations of temperamentally mismated partners. Norma, the salesgirl, exemplifies a sphere of life in which the business slogan that "the customer is right" has demonstrated its effectiveness as a bar to temperamental outbursts. In subsequent lectures the tempermental tangle in the marital relationship between Tom and Margaret will be reviewed, and instead of furnishing an exclusively didactic analysis of the problems inherent in temperamental behavior the temperamentally-acting persons themselves will be presented. That a concrete treatment of this kind is superior to a theoretical analysis is obvious and needs no special recommendation.

LECTURE 11

THE TEMPERAMENTAL PREDISPOSITION

If, in a crowded street car, the man by your side steps on your corn you feel intense pain and are likely to turn on the offender with fury. If the same corn is "stepped on" by an accidentally falling stone the pain may be just as intense or even of greater intensity but your temper has no offender to descend on. With the man you lose your temper, with the stone you control it.

I shall quote another example: if your six-year-old boy makes a rash pass in the direction of a cup, spilling its contents over the clean table cloth, your temper may explode. If the same cup is pushed over by the clumsy move of your one-year-old infant you are pained by the effect but not provoked into an outburst. Again, with the older boy you lose your temper, with the baby you control it.

Men With Explosive Tempers Suspect Others
of Evil Intentions and Lack of
Consideration

You may have a ready explanation for the differential treatment of the stone and the baby, on the one hand, and the man and the boy on the other. You may argue that the man and the boy, possessed of reasoning power, could have prevented the accident. They could have shown better consideration for the sensibilities of others and could have exercised greater care in moving and acting. In other words, you indict them for lack of consideration, or perhaps for evil intentions. Of course, stones and babies cannot reasonably be expected to show consideration or to have intentions, good or evil. Stones and babies produce effects by accident; adult persons and older children are judged by different standards. They are supposed to act deliberately and intentionally. Of the latter you expect behavior guided by friendly intentions or, at least, by proper consideration, while the former are exempt from such expectations.

I used the word "expectation" and meant to imply that whether you check or release your temper depends on how you expect others to behave. The man in the street car did not live up to your expectation. When he failed to do so you instantly suspected him of inconsiderateness or, worse yet, of unfriendly intentions. From this you may learn that you approach your fellow men with well formulated *expectations* which may turn into equally well formulated *suspicions* after your expectations have been disappointed. The conclusion is plain: men with explosive tempers expect too much consideration from their fellows and view their motives and intentions with too much suspicion.

When the man in the street car made that fatal "misstep" which brought him into contact with your toe your expectation was disappointed and your suspicion aroused. Your wife tried to calm you. "The man couldn't help it," she said, "the street car stopped suddenly and the jolt made him lose balance and threw him against you. He didn't do it intentionally; it was just an accident." You see, your wife's expectations were not disappointed and her suspicions were not aroused. The same was true of the men and women in the aisles and seats who witnessed the occurrence. Both they and your wife took the *objective attitude* that an accident had happened, while you experienced the *subjective disposition* to suspect an offender of evil intentions.

Misinterpretation of Injury as Insult Is Condoned as in Accord With "Human Nature"

The men and women, including your wife, who observed your temperamental outburst did not approve of it. They condemned your manner of "jumping at a conclusion" and were critical of your judgment. However they were not shocked or scandalized by your demeanor. Why should they be? What you did was unmannered and regrettable but, nevertheless, in perfect accord with what is commonly thought to be "human nature." According to this doctrine of "human nature," it is *perfectly natural* to pounce on a man who steps on your corn, to turn with fury on your son who spills the coffee, to fume against the waiter who, in a time-bound world must take his time to serve you and to fulminate against the bus driver if the chatter of the riders prevents him from hearing the buzz of your stop signal. In all these instances, pain or inconvenience was caused you by sheer accident and misinterpreted by your suspicious disposition as malicious intent. Your suspicion was unjustified and your disposition unbecoming but precisely the thing to be expected, "human nature being what it is."

What with a dash of facetiousness and a good deal of cynicism is called "human nature" is nothing but what I have frequently described as the "subjective disposition" as opposed to the "objective attitude." A child striking his leg against the chair, cries out in pain and lashes out furiously against the "offending" piece of furniture. The objective damage is subjectively felt as provocation, the injury as insult, the cause as motive, the innocent accident as hostile intent. Gradually the child learns that inanimate objects have no intentions and, as the years pass, he is not likely to release his temper when "opposed" by inert matter. When he now dashes his head against the stove he feels the pain but takes the "objective attitude" that no intention is involved and no retaliation called for.

The Child Senses the Intention of "Others" as Opposed to his Own Disposition

It is easy for the child to assume the objective attitude

toward lifeless objects and to realize that they do not hurt him intentionally. But the hurts inflicted on him by his parents are too frequent and too systematically practiced to be passed off as not meant or not intended. Father and mother do as they please, and if they want a cookie they just take it and nobody interferes. But let him do the same and he is sure to be reminded, energetically and deliberately, that eating between meals is not permitted. He advances hunger as a "perfectly natural" reason for his desire, but the argument is brushed aside with utter lack of consideration for his "natural disposition." That disposition of his is constantly offended, provoked, insulted and intentionally disregarded. He is right now disposed to play with his toys but is compelled to go to bed and to forego his pleasure. He just "feels like" tearing a page out of father's book but is severely censured and perhaps even spanked. Everyone in the house strikes a match as he chooses, or opens the window as he wishes, but he is prohibited from even touching a match or crawling on the sill. The world in which he lives is one in which his "natural" disposition is given no consideration and where his "perfectly human" desires are deliberately and systematically thwarted.

The boy does not know what the words "disposition" and "intention" mean. But he is fully aware that if he wants something the chances are the "others" will not want him to get it. He does not know what is the meaning of "discrimination." But there is no doubt that the "others" can do as they please and he cannot. The "others" talk to their heart's delight and nobody bids them to be silent. But if he goes on one of his fond talking sprees he is likely to be rudely interrupted. The "others" receive polite answers to their questions, but when he asks why the rain is wet and why the little piggies have no nurse he is brusquely told to keep quiet when father is speaking. It is all too plain that the "others" are set against him. They want him to be a good boy and intend to make him behave.

But what they call "good" is precisely what he dislikes and what they consider "naughty" is just what gives him supreme delight. Their views and thoughts are always in the way of his likes and joys. Their intentions invariably cross his disposition.

In time he conceives a thorough distaste for their intentions and delights in displaying his disposition. They want him to eat "like a nice boy," and he knows what that means. It means that he must sacrifice his wishes to their will. He knows that from recent experience. Yesterday he spilled the soup and smeared the potatoes over the table. It was done from disposition, not from malice. But father's ire was aroused and the boy was threatened with punishment if that happened again. Today when the plate with soup is placed before him he is told to hold the spoon in the right hand and to see to it that nothing is spilled. But this is their intention, not his disposition. And ignoring their intention and following his disposition he loses no time jerking the spoon into the left hand, lustily splashing the soup over his suit and spreading the potatoes across the table. When the culprit refuses to yield he is pulled from the chair and placed in the corner against the wall. There he sulks and frets and his heart is full of hatred for father's intentions and replete with tender feelings for his own disposition.

The Rules of the Standard Interfere With the Child's Happiness and Relaxation

As development proceeds it becomes increasingly clear to the boy that the intentions of the "others" are meant to enforce rules and to uphold standards. He sees a crisp roll on father's plate and, without reflection or ceremony, reaches out for it. Instantly father's booming voice bawls at him, "You have to say 'please' if you want to take something." He is perplexed and at a loss to understand why he can't take the roll if he wants it and why he must say "please" if he does not at all feel like saying it. It is all foreign to his disposition, incomprehensible, mysterious and annoying. Finally, recovering from his initial bewilderment, he breathes forth a barely audible "please" and is given the roll. But the ordeal is not over yet. Father's eyes are still fixed on him, searchingly and citically: "Don't you know that you say 'thank you' if somebody gives you something?" Indeed, he ought to know by now. They tell him at every turn what he "has to do" and what he "must say" and what "can't" be done. He spills water and has to say "I am sorry"; if, after dinner, he is ready to leave the table he must first ask, "May I be excused, please?" When he utters the phrases they have a hollow ring. Their very sound is artificial, strange, unnatural. The phrases are not his; they do not flow from his disposition. They are imposed on him by an outside force which they call rules and standards.

Whenever he is in the company of adults he is exposed to the relentless pressure of the standard. His behavior must be good, his clothes clean, his face washed. They watch his looks, movements and speech and seldom find them conforming to the standard. Their unceasing vigilance makes him feel uncomfortable in their presence. He is relaxed and "himself" only when he plays with other children. When he is with the grown-ups he becomes restless, shifts his positions, changes his activities, "gets into everything" and—again—runs afoul of the standard. They scold him and he becomes more restless; the more restless he becomes the more he is likely to violate the standards. A fatal, irremediable vicious cycle ensues. The pressure of the standard creates restlessness; the restlessneess leads to violations. This produces greater pressure, intensified restlessness, renewed violations. There is no escape, no respite, no relaxation from the rigors of the standard.

The Child, as Hero, Angel and Victim, Fights the Adult Devils, Villains and Oppressors

The most agonizing feature about the standard is its senseless insistence on respect for the needs and feelings of others. In the morning he is awake in the early hours and has the natural desire to get up and play. But father sleeps and must not be disturbed. One of his delights is to don father's garments, particularly his hat and shoes. It somehow gives him the illusion of being a big man, and he is particularly fond of slipping his little feet into the giant shoes and stamping the floor with a heavy thud. But hardly has he made a few steps when mother or father or both rush at him, tearing the shoes from his feet and threatening a sound spanking should he ever dare put them on again. And all this fuss because the people downstairs don't like the noise. There is no end to the consideration that he must give to others. Mother takes him on an occasional visit to friends and he tries his favorite game of jumping on the furniture but is severely reprimanded because Aunt Joan "will not like that." On the street car he leans over and grabs the hat of the man in front of him. The man smiles but mother is frantic and threatens not to take him on rides any more if he doesn't stop bothering people. His own feelings count for nothing, the other person's feelings for everything. He does not understand the underlying principle but grasps instinctively without being able to formulate it that his inner feelings must be sacrificed to outside necessities. The necessities are those of the standard which demands that he check his *subjective disposition* and take the *objective attitude* that the others have a rightful claim to consideration.

Like every human being, our boy is addicted to the

common type of thought which is fond of exaggerations, generalizations and simplifications. To him, father is not firm but ruthless. In actual fact, he is frequently accorded freedom of action; indeed, his wishes are more often granted than denied. Nevertheless, he exaggerates his parents' attitude as one of cruel oppression and generalizes the occasional, or at best frequent, interventions into a perpetual, relentless exercise of tyranny. Finally, he simplifies his observations according to the familiar contrast pattern of angel—devil, hero—villain, victim—oppressor. He is the angel, hero and victim, the "others" are devils, villains, and oppressors. But father and mother are merely acting in the service of the standard, and it is the standard which is responsible for all the deviltry, villainy and oppression from which he suffers. He hates that standard and is prepared to fight it at every opportunity.

The Child's Many Dispositions Become Organized Into One Predisposition

Previously, when he was naughty he was so from disposition. That disposition was his born heritage and took its place alongside other dispositions. There was, for instance, the disposition to play, to pick up things from the floor and to put them in his mouth. Other dispositions were to handle objects, to look into them and to explore their contents. He liked to rummage in boxes, drawers and handbags, to dig in his nose, to imitate father's manner of sitting with arms crossed and legs extended. There was no end to the variety of dispositions stirring within his restless soul. But they were all of equal value; none had precedence over the other. They preceded or succeeded one another by the sheer accident of happening to be evoked by something occurring in the environment. At times he was busy inspecting his story book and when his eye happened to glance at a scrap of paper on the floor he dropped the book, picked up the paper and shoved it into his mouth.

There was no intent, no design to the order and succession with which one disposition was enacted after another. But now the hatred for the standard introduces rank, choice and preference into the chaos of dispositions. His dislike of the standard makes him favor those of his dispositions which are likely or certain to offend its rules. The dispositions are no longer haphazardly *arranged* waiting for a fortuitous occasion to bring them to realization; they are now *prearranged* in something like a battle formation. The *many dispositions* are mobilized under the command of *one predisposition*. Previously, he was sometimes naughty, sometimes well behaved. At times, he "felt like" swallowing dirt or scattering paper across the room; at other times he did not "feel like" doing so. But now he performs these acts, not because he likes or wants to do them, but merely in order to oppose the standard. The standard is his enemy, and he is forever prepared and predisposed to fight it.

To the Boy-Fighter Persons Are Enemies, and Objects, Ammunition

The boy is now a fighter. The persons around him are not conceived objectively as plain father and mother but, subjectively, as representatives of the hated standard, i.e., his enemies. Things around him are not plain objects but ammunition. Food, for instance, becomes a weapon with which to strike at the standard. He may be objectively hungry but refuses to eat in order to satisfy his subjective desire to antagonize the "standard bearers." In the evening, he may be objectively tired but is subjectively predisposed to oppose mother. So, in spite of his fatigue, he resists her efforts to put him to bed. What now determines his conduct is not the *objective attitude* but his *subjective predisposition*.

For many years he practices the subjective predisposition until it hardens into a set pattern. Then the educational forces begin to exert their influence. They teach him the virtues of cooperation with and consideration for the "others" and make him adopt the objective attitude. He cultivates the newly acquired pattern enthusiastically and wholeheartedly until it finally becomes his "second nature." But his "original nature" persists in the dark recesses of his inner organization. It is held back there and kept in leash but ready to break forth whenever an opportunity offers. As a rule, he now approaches people and events with his "second nature," i.e., with the objective attitude. But whenever he has a "just reason" for unleashing his "original nature" of the subjective predisposition he does so and again experiences the delight of fighting the "others" and striking formidable blows against the hated standard. The "just reason" is then conveniently supplied by the process of rationalization which I described in a previous lecture. (See page 132)

The Childish Predisposition of the Adult Man Waits for a "Just Cause" to Attack the Standard

We shall now revert to the incident of the man stepping on your corn. Of course, it was an accident, and the men and women who witnessed it, including your wife, instantly realized the accidental nature of the occurrence. Indeed, as things stood, evil intentions and ill will were the very last things to be considered. The man was a stranger to you. He did not even know your name. He never had any dealings with you, pleasant or unpleasant. He never had an opportunity to entertain feelings toward you, friendly or hostile. Even had he been your enemy was it reasonably probable that he would choose such a silly, childish and ineffective way of expressing his enmity? You see, there was not a shred of reason to assume that the man meant or intended to hurt your toe or your feelings. Why, then, did you explode?

The answer is that you are one of those individuals who, having grown up physically and intellectually, failed to mature emotionally. Physically and intellectually, you are a man, but emotionally, you are a child. As a child you approach people and events with your infantile predisposition and feel the irresistible urge to strike out against the standard of good behavior. As a child, you still suspect the "others" of evil intentions and refuse to take the objective attitude that certain things happen without being meant to hurt you. Of course, you have passed through courses of education and through the school of practical life and know that your secret desire to fight the standard must be curbed. But you are constantly waiting for an occasion which will give you a "just reason" to release your childish predisposition. Such occasions are presented when somebody innocently and accidentally steps on your corn, when the waiter is unavoidably delayed, when the bus driver fails to hear your signal, when your stenographer happens to make a mistake or when your wife has the misfortune to be late with the dinner. On all these and a thousand other occasions you have no objective reason for assuming an insult or offense but, driven on by your subjective predisposition, you rationalize the accident into an intention and are then "justified" in staging a counterattack. All of this is called temper and is thought to be "in perfect accord with human nature" which is correct except that the type of human nature that is involved is infantile rather than adult.

Temper Is a Habit, Nursed, Tended and Cultivated

Whatever quality you may assign to temper—infantile, predispositional, standard-opposed, rationalizing—the fact remains that it is nothing but a set of habits. And habits can be discarded, changed, revised, and many of them disappear spontaneously, undergo a process of disintegration and atrophy. If so, why is it so difficult to change or discard temperamental habits? The answer is that if a habit is the source of great pleasure it neither disappears spontaneously nor is it likely to be discarded. Smoking, drinking, gambling, theater going, sports activities and scores of other life-long habits are examples in point. They give great pleasure and, far from being discarded, are nursed and tended and cultivated until they become persistent, inveterate and deeply ingrained. Is temper a habit of this kind? Does it represent a source of great pleasure? Does the temperamental person nurse, tend and cultivate his temper? In order to give a satisfactory answer to the question I shall have to explain what is meant by the term "cultivating a habit."

Suppose you were in the habit, since early adolescence, of having coffee with every meal. But the physician orders a change in diet and prohibits the beverage. Most likely you will decide to discard the habit and will do so without undue difficulty. Then I shall know that the habit was of moderate strength and yielded a mere modicum of pleasure. Suppose now the physician levels his prohibition against your beer and cocktails which you imbide habitually in moderate quantities. You again decide to discard the habit, but this time you encounter considerable difficulty in carrying out your decision. My conclusion is that your drinking habit was strong and secured for you a great amount of pleasure. The pleasure which is provided made you cultivate it until it became firmly established.

Predispositions Are Nursed and Cultivated
Through Continued Endorsement and Approval

Remember the way your drinking habit worked. At noontime when you left your office to take lunch with your friends you knew beforehand that you would order meat, salad, and dessert. However, these courses were by no means looked forward to with keen antiticipation. You liked chops but were not "particularly keen" about them; you preferred shortcake to pie but the anticipation of the dish did not exhilarate you. This was different with the introductory cocktails and the subsequent sauterne which you were ready to imbibe. Their taste was already on your tongue when you merely thought about them. The mere anticipation of the drinks enlivened your spirits and stimulated your nerves. And thus anticipating the exercise of the fond habit you enjoyed it in advance and, incidentally, endorsed and approved of it. It is this manner of anticipating a habit with approval and endorsement which is most effective in nursing and cultivating it.

While the luncheon was in progress the drinks did not only delight you; you also gave enthusiastic expression to your delight; you did not tire extolling their excellence. When your friends complimented you on the exquisite flavor of the mixture which you recommended you felt proud of your reputation as connoisseur. Their praise added their endorsement and approval to yours. The habit thus received additional nursing and cultivating. After the luncheon was over the favorable comments continued. You were elated by the combined effect of the drinks and the flattery; your spirits sparkled when everybody raved about the "grand time" they had. In this manner, the *anticipation, immediate effect and after-effect* all contributed their share to the cultivation of the habit. After you returned to the office you reminisced, and in retrospect, the drinking—you called it conviviality—ranked in your mind as something desirable and beneficial. The habit now was accorded renewed approval and endorsement in recollection and reflection. The after-effect was reenforced. Originally, drinking was merely one of your dispositions. After the habit had been, on numerous occasions, looked forward to in thrilled anticipation, enjoyed in its immediate effect and rapturously reflected on in its after-effect it turned into a set and hardened predisposition. When the physician prohibited it you were asked to relinquish an inveterate and ingrained predisposition and found it very hard, indeed, to discard or change it. That predisposition had gathered unto itself such an amount of endorsement and approval that to abandon it meant to part with something cherished and valued.

Is the temperamental habit comparable to the habit of imbibing? Is it nursed, tended and cultivated by the same devices of anticipation, immediate effect and after-effect? Is it endorsed and approved of, similar to the drinking habit, by the temperamental person himself and by the tolerant or encouraging attitude of the public? The answer to these questions will be given in a subsequent series of lectures.

LECTURE 12

CULTIVATION AND REPUDIATION OF TEMPER

In my last lecture I discussed the temper outburst of the man whose corn was stepped on by another person in a crowded street car. We concluded that his temper was aroused by the fact that an innocent accident was misinterpreted as a deliberate offense. We further stated that the misinterpretation was not shared by the other passengers, including the wife of the temperamental hothead. They gave the correct interpretation to the meaning of the event and took the *objective attitude* that the incident was due to a chance happening rather than to an aggressive intention. On the other hand, the unfortunate victim of the collision failed to be objective and approached the occurrence with the *subjective disposition* to take revenge and to punish an offender.

In Trivial Mishaps the Onlooker Is Objective While the Sufferer Is Subjective

No doubt you often witnessed similar scenes in which toes were hurt and tempers exploded. The spectacle is always the same; the injured person acts on his subjective disposition while the onlookers take the objective attitude. Our sufferer—we shall call him Joe—was frequently an onlooker himself and as such invariably retained his objectivity. There was never a doubt in his mind on such occasions that the suffering inflicted on others was accidental. The thought of an offense did not occur to him and he always marvelled at the temperamental agitation which people are likely to display when a "sore spot" of theirs was touched by a sheer accident.

151

Other men's experiencees he viewed objectively, his own subjectively.

Had any of the onlookers been in Joe's place be certain they would have acted Joe's part. Their objectivity would have wilted, their subjectivity would have soared to the heights of temperamental violence. You see, it is "human nature" to be calm and objective in the case of a trivial mishap which involves your fellow and to become emotional and subjective if the same trivial mishap affects your own "self." The other man's "self" is viewed objectively and rationally, your own "self" subjectively and irrationally.

Everybody Is a Dual Personality With a Dual Viewpoint

You do not have to wait for a shakeup in a street car in order to observe the dual character of "human nature." In the peaceful precinct of your own privacy you can make similar observations; if your daughter or maid breaks a dish you become enraged at their carelessness; if the breakage happens to you it is an accident which is instantly dismissed from your mind without comment. Your guest's late arrival is inexcusable and "just an outrage," while your own failure to be on time is unfortunate and unavoidable. If your fence is damaged by the neighbor's little son you burn with indignation at the atrocious manner in which "some people bring up their children." If the damage is done by your own boy to the neighbor's fence you excuse the act on the grounds that "Charlie is just a child and doesn't know what he is doing." In the case of an offense committed by another person, your subjective predisposition is always ready to condemn; in your case, your objective attitude is ready to condone. You are—and everybody seems to be—a dual personality with a dual viewpoint. At times you advance the subjective viewpoint and become emotional and temperamental; at other times the objective viewpoint is favored and emotion and temper are controlled. "It all depends on the way you look on things," and your temper will have free rein if you cultivate the subjective way of looking at things while it will be kept in reasonable control if the objective view of things is given the right of way.

The Average Person Is Unaware of Approving and Endorsing Temper

Your viewpoint is a set of habits and as such subject to the process of nursing, tending and cultivating which I described in a previous lecture. (See page 149) You remember I told you that a habit is cultivated by the approval and endorsement which it receives in anticipation, immediate effect and after effect. But you will immediately protest that your temper outbursts come upon you unheralded and unexpected. They are, you think, the response to a provocation which, as a rule, was not foreseen. And as to the approval and endorsement which you are supposed to confer on your temper you will enter a most strenuous denial. Why, you certainly do not brag about your fits nor do you boast of your rages. As far as you are concerned you are wholly unaware of your approving or endorsing.

The Temperamental Street Car Rider

In reply to your protest I shall remind you of a recent experience when the street car conductor "had the nerve" to challenge the validity of your transfer ticket. You insisted on continuing the trip without paying another fare and staged a violent argument. This was a temper outburst. But was it anticipated? There was undoubtedly the immediate effect of fury and indignation. Yon do not deny that. And after you finally yielded and paid the additional fare you were certainly aflame with resentment over the "unheard-of outrage." This was the after-effect, and you do not deny that either. But why speak of approval and endorsement? There was no time to think, judge or reflect. The thing overpowered you; you were thrown into a fit of anger and "could not help" exploding; it all happened spontaneously, was neither staged deliberately nor anticipated, approved or endorsed. What actually took place was an occurrence that is common enough. In the interim between transferring from one car to the other you entered the dime store to buy a toy for your child. The aisles were packed with people and you had to "worm" your way slowly to the counter. The salesgirl was busy and kept you waiting. In the end, you had spent fully twenty minutes on the purchase. On the way out you met a neighbor and "couldn't just run out on her." So you had a friendly chat and, in the process, rounded out a full half hour's waiting time. You will remember that while hurrying back to the corner you worried about the conductor's reaction. You feared to be challenged and armed yourself hastily with suitable excuses and explanations. Do you realize that you anticipated a fight and were primed for an explosion?

Mark that in this instance you knew you were wrong and the conductor was right. You knew that you had exceeded the allotted time and had forfeited the use of the ticket. You simply permitted yourself to commit one of those petty frauds which are thoroughly reprehensible and deplorable but somehow sanctioned by widespread usage. But in spite of the fact that you knew you were wrong you worked yourself up to a feverish pitch, assailed the conductor with heat and indignation and fought a ferocious battle for your rights, presumably for your "sacred rights." Do you now understand that when you defended your rights you endorsed your emotion and approved of your temper? The mere fact that you insisted on being right gave approval to your procedure. You endorsed your own viewpoint and condemned that of the conductor.

Endorsement and Approval Pervade Every Phase
of Temperamental Reaction

When you finally decided to pay the additional fare and took your seat inside the car you were still ablaze with excitement. A burning desire for revenge raged within you. You were going to write a letter to the company "the very first thing" you arrived home. And you were not going to mince words, either. You fairly revelled in the thought of "getting even" with that impossible conductor. And, in this stage of the after-effect, you not only endorsed and approved of your temper but anticipated another temperamental delight when you thought of the letter you were going to dispatch.

You see, endorsement and approval pervade and penetrate every phase of your temperamental reaction and give their distinctive coloring to anticipation, immediate effect and after-effect. In giving their sanction they nurse, tend and cultivate your temperamental *disposition* until, through unceasing cultivation, it hardens into a set predisposition which becomes firmly intrenched in your innermost organization.

If temper is cultivated and perpetuated by continuous endorsement it is obvious that in order to eliminate temper a way must be found to eliminate endorsement. What you endorse in a temperamental act of behavior is its justification, reasonableness and propriety. In your altercation with the street car conductor you endorsed and justified your expected bout during the stage of anticipation when you prepared your excuses and explanation. To explain means to justify, to excuse means to endorse. Your endorsement became vehement and impetuous when, during the stage of the immediate effect, you insisted with fervor that you were right and the conductor wrong. Endorsement almost climaxed into a passion for righteousness when, during the after-effect, you fairly burst with indignation at the outrage of which you fancied yourself the innocent victim.

Treating Temper Means Treating After-Effect

Clearly, in order to check your temperamental disposition you will have to eliminate endorsement and justification. But it would be futile to concentrate your corrective effort on the immediate effect. During that stage your blood boils, your pulse hammers, and reasoning and reflection are all but wiped out. Every effort at control is here wasted. The stage of anticipation is similarly unfavorable for the practice of control. In our example with the street car conductor, anticipation was conscious, plain and palpable and might perhaps have lent itself to successful treatment. But ordinarily, anticipation is a subtle process, largely hidden from conscious perception and not easily analyzed. The only stage which offers itself as suitable occasion for the practice of control is the after-effect. If this is correct the problem of treating temper resolves itself into the question of how to deal with the after-effect.

At Home Norma Nursed, Tended and Cultivated Temperamental Disposition

You remember my description of the dual reaction of Norma, the salesgirl. (See page 125) When Norma was behind the counter she controlled her temper with consummate skill, but at home that same temper was released with the utmost lack of self discipline. With customers she practiced the objective attitude, with her mother she displayed the subjective disposition. The dual reaction appears baffling and mysterious but is easily explained on the basis of a dual treatment of the after-effect. One day, on coming home in the evening, Norma found that the dress which she was eager to wear at a dinner engagement that night had not yet arrived from the cleaner. She turned on her mother with violent accusations, fumed and raged and made the home a scene of madness. After a while she left and took a bus to the place where she was to meet her boy friend Charles. During the ride she had ample time to go over in her mind every detail of the commotion she had caused at home. The picure of the mother crying and sobbing was before her. She could not forget the frightened and pleading look in the old lady's eyes, her haggard features and the sad expression of helplessness and resignation. And Norma fell into a pensive mood. For the flicker of a moment she sensed the unnecessary rudeness of her behavior and winced under the impact of a guilty conscience. But in another instant she shook off doubt and self-criticism and the softness which for a few seconds had stolen over her face gave way to a look of set determination. And forthwith, during the entire length of the bus trip, she indulged in an orgy of justification, approval and endorsement. True, she caused her mother a great deal of suffering, worry and sleeplessness. Perhaps she could be more lenient and less irritable. But good heavens, there was plenty of irritation with the customers at the store, and a girl coming home after a strenuous day cannot help being nervous and a mother ought to know that. After taking all the abuse from insulting customers was she not entitled to some consideration at home? And contributing a good part of her salary to the family budget had she no right to demand some service? That was nothing but fair exchange and if mother, in her old fashioned ways, didn't grasp that simple fact, well, there will be more spats and more arguments and mother will have nobody to blame but herself. You see, during the stage of the after-effect Norma gave full endorsement and approval to her temper outburst when she mused that "if mother didn't . . . well there *will be* more spats and more arguments and mother *will have* nobody to blame but herself." She anticipated already renewed temper outbursts and gave them endorsement and approval in advance. And while thus piling endorsement and approval on renewed anticipation she nursed and tended and cultivated her temper and perpetuated her subjective predisposition.

At the Store Norma Repudiated and Condemned Temperamental Reactions

At times—on very rare occasions—Norma lost her temper with a customer. One instance stood out with particular force in her memory. A lady asked to be shown handbags. Norma was polite and sweet but her patience was put to an almost unbearable test. The woman, a shrivelled spinster of notoriously mean disposition, was rude in the extreme and expressed her dissatisfaction in such insulting remarks as "I don't see why you show me nothing but trash. Have they no experienced girls in this store? Why, a girl of your age ought to have better taste than that. . . . " Finally, Norma could not contain herself and retorted, "You don't have to buy, Madam, if you don't like the bag." Whereupon the acid remark, "I don't need your advice, young lady, and it wouldn't do you any harm to acquire better manners." The atmosphere was tense, the lady growing more insulting, Norma more impatient. Finally, there was biting reference to "poor breeding," "lack of common sense" and "girls without proper upbringing." The last insinuation finally unnerved Norma who snapped back, "You don't have to buy but I don't have to stand for your insults." The lady rushed to the floorman, registered a complaint against that "most unmannered person" and Norma was called before the manager and duly censured. All during that afternoon her cheeks burned with shame and rage and her body shook with indignation. In intervals between serving customers she had time to reflect on the incident. Oh, she could just kill that nasty hag. But, of course, it was a customer, and the manager was right in reprimanding her for the rash reply. Alas, a salesgirl had to know how to take it. And next time, be sure, she was going to be courteous no matter how ugly and sarcastic and insulting the customer may be. You see, in her role of a salesgirl, Norma did not give approval and endorsement to her explosions, and the after-effect was not utilized for the purpose of justifying the propriety and reasonableness of outbursts. Instead of endorsing her temperamental habits and viewpoints she repudiated and condemned them. She did that both in the after-effect and in the anticipation of the next occasion when a similar contingency should arise.

Endorsement of After-Effect Anticipates Renewed Outburst

The two illustrations which I offered ought to demonstrate clearly that it is during the stage of the after-effect that temper can be either cultivated or inhibited. If during that stage you endorse your preceding explosion your predisposition for other explosions is strengthened. The sense of "having been right" clothes your temper in a halo of righteousness and places a premium on the next outburst. Without being clearly aware of it you are already primed for the forthcoming opportunity when you might again experience that exhilarating feeling of "being right" or "having been right." The endorsement of the after-effect and the subsequent anticipation of a renewed outburst combine to cultivate the temperamental habit and to make it well nigh ineradicable. On the other hand, if temper is repudiated in the after-effect there will be no anticipation of the next explosion except in horror—and cultivation of the habit will be avoided.

I have told you repeatedly that temper is practically no problem in social contacts. It hardly ever happens that you "forget yourself" when you are invited on the outside or when you have guests at home; nor do you ever dare "forget yourself" with your superiors or with important people anywhere. Of course, what the term "important" precisely means to you is difficult to state. But be certain that if keeping on good terms with the neighbors looms as an "important" task in your mind your temper will not be permitted free explosions against them. And if your employees are more than mere "hired men"; if the quality and continuity of their service count as "important" items in the list of your business assets, you will never or seldom "forget yourself" in dealing with them. If this is true, what is needed for conquering temper is not to "forget" the "importance" of situations. Why, then, did I offer such complex rules for temper control as withholding approval and endorsement during and after the various states of the explosions? Would it not be a far simpler procedure to call to your mind the "importance" of domestic peace and to urge you not to "forget yourself" in the presence of wife, husband, father, mother, son and daughter?

The Returned Patient Must Be Protected From Continued Eruptions and Explosions

I do not have to tell you that domestic peace ought to occupy a most "important" place in the mind of every member of the family. However, the fact is that its "importance" is generally ignored or overloooked. You know the reason: if you "forget yourself" on the outside you incur the danger of ostracism and social isolation, while at home your forgetfulness carries no penalty. Present day public opinion sees to it that you exercise the utmost vigilance in your public and semi-public relations but is indifferent to your family relations. If public opinion insisted on your being as much on your guard with the members of your family as you are with strangers and friends domestic temper would no longer be the grave issue that it is today. You would simply refrain from staging temperamental scenes. None but the simplest rules would be sufficient to check your wild outbursts. You would merely have to keep in mind that not only customers, office clerks, union laborers and neighbors but also the members of your own family "are always right" in those trivialities which customarily arouse temper. If this rule were backed by the force of determined public opinion your home would be as perennially peaceful as are the average office, salesroom, grocery store and bakery shop. But this would include the entire round of your daily activities and your temper would have no sphere left upon which to play. You would be an angel, freed of the last remnant of your "human nature." I am not sufficiently naive and visionary to anticipate the very possibility of such ideal circumstances and take it for granted that "human nature being what it is" you will continue exploding and "forgetting yourself" at home in spite of all the golden rules which I may be able to devise for you. Knowing the obstinacy and conservatism of "human nature" I do not for a moment think of asking you to eliminate your temperamental disposition. All I ask you is not to nurse, tend and cultivate it until it hardens into an inveterate predisposition. This you can do by withholding approval and endorsement during the stage of the temperamental after-effect. If you do that, the recovered patient, after leaving the hospital, will return to a home which, while not free from temperamental outbursts, will not be continually rocked by fierce eruptions and violent explosions.

LECTURE 13

THE ILLUSION OF SUPERIORITY

Tom recovered and was sent home to his wife Margaret. When, after several months, he returned to the hospital for a visit, he appeared to be in good mental health but somewhat subdued and tense. He was reticent and evasive, insisting there was "nothing wrong" with him. Finally, the physician succeeded in piloting him into a more communicative mood whereupon the familiar story of marital misunderstanding and domestic discord unfolded itself.

What the patient reported was by no means a record of violent explosions and uncontrolled outbursts. Margaret's language was mild and her manner courteous Indeed, her verbal utterance overflowed with a gush of endearing appellations ranging from the plain "dad" and "dear" to the more effusive and affectionate "honey" and "sweetheart." Unfortunately, sweetness and tenderness were reserved for verbal expression only. In the field of action, Margaret was domineering, impatient, scheming and relentlessly pressing for the granting of her pet and petty demands.

Margaret Dominated Tom by Means
of Migraine Headache

Margaret's main means of dominating Tom was a migraine headache. She was likely to rouse Tom in the dead of the night and to keep him awake with endless wails and complaints. On such occasions, she maintained a steady flow of requests for icecaps and aspirin, for rearranging the pillows and changing the ice in the bag. If the services were not executed with the expected rapidity a torrent of criticism was loosed on the hapless husband.

Tom was co-partner with his brother Edward in a moderately prosperous laundry establishment. At times he served customers; at other times he superintended the work in the plant or conferred with salesmen. In this manner he was busy all day, and Margaret knew well how busy he was as she was familiar with the business routine from the days when she had helped in the shop. In spite of this knowledge she was in the habit of telephoning Tom two or three times a day, belaboring him with extended accounts of her "unbearable" suffering and keeping him at the telephone for fifteen or twenty minutes. When Tom pleaded lack of time on the score of customers waiting to be served Margaret retorted, with a display of bitterness, "Of course, you always have excuses. What do you care if your wife goes through agonies of pain? As far as you are concerned, I may as well rot away and die." Tom, softhearted and sympathetic, was conscience stricken and for weeks did not dare interrupt his wife's endless telephone communications.

"Allergy" Was the Excuse for Unreasonable Demands

I shall quote a few other examples of Margaret's behavior. As is common with migraine sufferers, Margaret was also afflicted with hay fever. Indeed, the migraine and the hay fever were merely different symptoms of one and the same ailment which all of you know by the name of allergy. The word "allergy" was not used by Margaret's physician at the time when she merely complained of the headache. It was only after the hay fever developed that the term "allergy" was heard in Tom's home. But then it became a household word and was used, with increasing frequency, as topic of conversation, subject of complaint and, most important, as a ready excuse for unreasonable demands and for neglect of duty. Of course, Margaret demanded the yearly "hay-fever season" in Wisconsin in order to escape the pollen-infested air of Chicago. This was perhaps her due privilege, and could hardly be called unreasonable. But when, out of season, she timed her allergic attacks to coincide, with almost devilish regularity, with Tom's period of recreation, the timing was certainly difficult to understand. All Tom had to do was to plan a week-end hunting trip,, and an allergic spell was sure to be expected for the coming Saturday. The wife's allergy was likely to keep him from attending conventions, meetings, football games and any kind of social gathering or sports activities. That the allergic discharges, pains, itches and rashes served as current excuses for neglecting meals and other household duties was more understandable but equally disturbing.

Tom bore with his wife's complaints and did what he could to accommodate her. But lately Margaret went to intolerable extremes in interfering with her husband's routine on the score of her allergy. One day she discovered that she was allergic to Tom's shaving soap and to the brand of cold cream he used. She then insisted that he cease shaving at home. Eager to preserve the last remnant of domestic peace that had survived the wife's eccentricities, Tom actually moved his shaving utensils to his office and finished his daily toilet in front of partner and employees. There, however, he was exposed to leering glances and taunting remarks and felt mortified. It was at this stage of his marital distress that he felt the need for a heart-to-heart talk with his physician.

Margaret Was Blind to What Everybody Saw

After hearing the story of Tom and Margaret, not one of you will be in doubt as to the meaning of Margaret's behavior. Plainly, she made use of an ailment in order to dominate her husband. But if meanings and motives are so plainly transparent and simple, how is it that Margaret, a woman of native intelligence and fair school instruction, was *blind* to the significance of her reactions? When Tom transferred his shaving activity to his office everyone there immediately *saw* the underlying reasons. The delivery boys were surprised, Tom's secretary was painfully sympathetic, and the older employees who ranked as his chums and pals took the liberty, together with his brother Edward, to pass jocular remarks at the newly introduced oddity in shaving procedure. The surprise, the sympathy and the joking were all meant to condemn the wife's domineering manner. If they saw, why was Margaret blind? It was not a matter of intellect; in this, Margaret was equal if not superior to delivery boy, secretary and partner. Nor was it a matter of breeding and manners because Margaret was by no means deficient in these qualities, as evidenced by her general conduct. The puzzle seems to deepen; if Margaret possessed intellect, manners and breeding, why was she *blind* to the meaning of reactions the grotesqueness of which were *visible* to everybody else?

Convenient Blindness Preserves
Petty Illusions

That people are blind to the meaning of reactions is a common experience. Think of the lover whose love makes him blind to the shortcomings of his idol. If the woman of whom he is enamored lies to him he ignores the deception. You say he does not see facts because he is blindly in love. But is he really blind? Of course he is not. He merely refuses to see or hear what his eyes or ears present to him as incontrovertible evidence. As a matter of fact, the lover is afraid to see anything that might mar the delights of his infatuation. He shuts his eyes because some sights might be shocking to him. You see here that in situations of this kind blindness is a means of escaping shocks, disappointments and disillusionment. Similar examples of convenient blindness are most common in the relationship between mothers and sons. A son frequently refuses to see his mother's defects, and a mother is apt to blind herself deliberately to the son's failings. To exercise sight would destroy fond delusions and pet ambitions. Hence the determination to shut out the sights and to practice blindness. The average son entertains the illusion that his mother is a paragon of sweetness. If in actual fact her behavior is that of a nagging, scheming and sour person the son may refuse to see the undesirable traits in order to save his favorite illusion. In these instances, blindness is nothing but an unwillingness to see and serves the purpose of preserving the charm and inspiration of an illusion.

Self-Importance Is the Most Common Illusion

Everybody has illusions and in order to save them refuses to see facts which are apt to destroy or weaken them. The most common illusion is that of one's own "self" being important. Daily occurrences demonstrate to everybody how relatively unimportant is his "self." Everybody has frequently observed how his plans miscarry, how his judgment fails him in vital decisions, how emotion gets the better of his intellect and how his resolutions are mocked by his impulses. All in all, human beings are too frequently victims instead of victors, frail instead of sturdy, erring instead of succeeding. Nevertheless, the illusion of self-importance is maintained against the evidence of facts. Should the facts and their evidence be looked at, the individual would discover his shortcomings and gain insight into his basic weakness. The insight would be shocking and disillusioning. In order to forestall the shock of disillusionment the individual silences the voice of insight and blocks its function.

Margaret Secured a Sense of Superiority by Treating Tom as Inferior

To a certain extent, the sense of importance is a desirable quality because it is the basis of self-confidence and self-respect. Unfortunately, many people confuse importance with superiority. Margaret was a wife and as such important to Tom. In addition, she was important as a daughter to her mother and as a sister to her brothers. In all likelihood, she was also important as friend, as member of clubs, as neighbor, etc. This, however, was not sufficient food for her boundless ambition. She craved superiority. Her life was that of the average person, with the average frustrations and difficulties. If she viewed the naked facts of her daily existence her attainments could be rated as fair average or good average but not as superior. A person impelled by the sense of superiority cannot tolerate the idea of being "just average." The average existence which Margaret was forced to lead was a challenge to her illusion of superiority. She had to prove that she was *not average*; she had perforce to demonstrate that she was superior. Superiority is best demonstrated by the fact that others are inferior. This can hardly be done with strangers, friends, and neighbors. They would effectively thwart any attempt to prove them inferior. Proof of this kind is more easily obtained from close relatives, mothers, fathers, husbands and wives. Tom was an ideal object for target practice. He was meek, patient and peace loving. He shrank instinctively from fights and was content to have the worst of an argument. With qualities of this kind, it was easy to place him in a position of seeming inferiority. All Margaret had to do in order to establish her claim to superiority was to criticize his statements, to interrupt him rudely when he related a story or to order him about with a commanding voice. The mere fact that Tom submitted without resistance was proof positive that she was superior and he inferior. In all these domestic skirmishes. Margaret was almost invariably the victor, Tom the victim. At home, her claim to superiority seemed to be founded on a rock of convincing evidence.

Unfortunatelly for Margaret's ambition, her claim to superiority, so securely established at home, was rudely challenged abroad. Her social status was average, her gifts and talents mediocre, nothing outstanding, nothing exceptional. Occasionally she was offered the post of a secretary in a local club or an assignment in Sunday school work, but leadership and exalted rank were denied her. True, at home she was not superior, either; she merely created the illusion of superiority by treating Tom as her inferior. But on the outside there was no possibility of treating others as inferior. There she was *just average*.

Superiority Is Very Rare Quality

I shall have to digress here and say a few words about superiority and averageness. You may know a general in the army and the president of a large corporation and the editor of an important newspaper and an internationally known opera singer. If you proclaim them superior I shall ask you to whom they are superior. I grant that the general is or may be superior to many majors and colonels serving in his army. But is he superior to other generals? The same question may be asked about the opera star. She is doubtless superior to vaudeville performers and to singers in her own cast with less brilliance of voice. But how does she rank among other international stars? Can she maintain superiority among them, too? If you give your question the proper wording and ask whether a person is superior or exceptional if compared to other persons of similar attainments you will realize that superiority is a quality that is reserved to very few human beings. Should you comb the entire sweep of recorded history you would hardly be able to list more than a few hundred who will qualify as truly superior. Superiority, in other words, is a very rare condition and, implying exceptionality, is exceptionaal indeed. The great mass of humanity is of course not superior but average. Take the example of a recognized specialist in any field of medicine. Suppose he is a well-known surgeon. Measured by the attainments of the group of recognized surgeons he can congratulate himself if, among them, he is rated as *good average*. If his classification were that of *fair average* his place within his group would still be a credit to him.

To Be "Just Average" Was an Intolerable Thought to Margaret

From what I told you, you will be able to infer that superiority is nothing but an illusion. I shall add: the most common illusion. You will recall that when I discussed the development of the child I described the so-called normal youngster as one who feels superior to everybody and everything. I stated at the time that the overwhelming majority of children adjust their original craving for superiority and gradually settle down to an average existence. In shedding their exaggerated sense of superiority they go through a process of growth and maturation. Some children never mature. They carry with them their sense of superiority through adolescence into adult life and, having no genuine claim to the title defend it with all the more tenacity. Margaret never matured. She never abondoned her immoderate yearning for superiority. The reason why she failed to reach maturity was that she was brought up by a mother with boundless ambition.

Margaret was the youngest of four children. Her mother, unhappily married, and disappointed in life, pinned all her hopes on the children's happiness. Margaret was her favorite. The child had charm and beauty and was moderately talented. The mother dreamed of her as a future star and whipped up the dauthter's energies in the direction of stardom. The meager family resources were badly strained in the effort to secure first-class instruction in music, dancing, and dramatics. The results were unsatisfactory and the teachers offered little encouragement; but the mother, bent on pursuing her goal, pushed Margaret along on the road to fame and fortune. When Margaret reached adolescence her mind was geared to the idea of greatness but her talents had not developed measurably beyond the stage of mediocrity. She did not figure in the headlines, nor did her stage performances attract impressive audiences. Life presented to her the incontrovertible evidence of averageness, but her lively imagination, abetted by an unreasonably ambitious mother, nursed the illusion of superiority. To be "just average" was an intolerable thought to her. And if life demonstrated her averageness she was determined to prove that, far from being average, she was, indeed, superior.

Superiority of Force Mistaken For Superiority of Attainment

The problem which faced Margaret was plainly this: her daily activities were of an average nature; her husband, her family, her social group were of average status. How could she, in this limitless sea of averageness, prove that she was the only isolated rock of superiority? Since the thought of being "nothing but average" was intolerable to her she had perforce to give conclusive evidence of superiority. But how could she prove superiority if she was not graced with even a modicum of this divine gift?

The human mind has the fatal capacity to twist meanings and, through successful juggling of words and concepts, to create illusions. Superiority is one of the concepts that lend themselves to skillfull juggling. Its original and authentic meaning is superior attainment or *genius*. Another meaning, however, is superior force or greater (physical, social, or economic) *power*. Margaret was not in a position to prove her genius. But she could conveniently demonstrate her power over her meek and submissive husband. By bossing and bullying Tom she wielded power and created the illusion of superiority.

While exercising and enjoying her illusion of superiority Margaret painfully discovered the weakness common to illusions in general: they are easily looked through. The human mind has many capacities and one of the most distressing is the capacity to look at one's "self." When a human being looks into his "self" he inspects its nature, its claims, and pretenses and, in the process, scrutinizes and criticizes their value. He then gains insight into the value or valuelessness of his "self." If the "self" is crowded with illusions insight is apt to weaken or destroy them. In other words: insight is the foe of illusion; it is disillusioning.

The "Self" Is Represented by Thoughts, Feelings and Actions

It did not take long for Margaret to discover that in order to enjoy fully the delights of marital power politics (to her it meant superiority) she had to avoid looking at her "self." Of course, nobody can really look at one's "self." I cannot enter into a detailed discussion of this subject, but you all know that what we call the "self" is nothing concrete; it is a thing in the abstract; it cannot be seen or heard or felt. However, the "self" is expressed or manifested (1) in one's thoughts, (2) in one's feelings, (3) in one's actions. When Margaret became aware of or noticed or "looked at" her thoughts, feelings and actions, she beheld the representatives of her "self." Were they valuable? Did they have the marks of superiority?

When the average man and woman look at their thoughts they have no difficulty maintaining the illusion of a valuable "self." The vast majority of their thoughts are worthy, sympathetic, perhaps even lofty and generous. Even if thoughts of petty scheming, ugly suspicions or harsh intentions obtrude themselves into consciousness the picture as a whole remains that of a "generally valuable self." Moreover, most thoughts of an ethically or morally doubtful nature have a way of merely flitting through the brain without leaving much of a trace. With regard to feelings the situation is pretty much the same. With the average person, the majority of feelings are worthy and commendable, perhaps even noble and lofty and expressive of a "generally valuable self." It is true that feeelings do not have the tendency merely to flit through the organism. They have greater intensity and duration. But this is compensated for by the fact that the average person who becomes aware of reprehensible feelings and impulses has a well-developed technique of justifying them. A wife feeling a sudden surge of hatred or resentment against her husband has no difficulty, as a rule, convincing her "self" that it is the husband's responsibility if she cannot feel otherwise.

Margaret Had to Block Insight Into the Meaning of Her Actions

Had the value of her "self" depended on thoughts and feelings only, Margaret would have experienced no difficulty maintaining the illusion of a valuable "self." Unfortunately, it depended on her actions also. This difference between actions on the one hand, and thoughts and feelings, on the other, will be clear to you if, for a brief moment, you will consult your own experience. How often did you have the feeling "I could kill that person?" Perhaps thousands of times. For the moment, you actually had some sort of a "murderous" impulse. Nevertheless, you never thought of your "self" as a potential murderer. I need not tell you how different that would be if, on only one such occasion, you had actually grabbed a gun or swung a knife. There would have seen no actual shooting or stabbing; nothing but a movement of your arm in the direction of the weapon. Nevertheless your "self" would stand indicted. Its value would be damaged or destroyed. This example illustrates that frequently one single action may be fatal to the value of the "self." You will now understand that Margaret, in her desire to preserve the illusion of her valuable and superior "self," could safely afford to look at her thoughts and feelings. But with regard to her actions she had to be on guard. If the sight of her actions was likely to deny or question the superiority of her "self" it was imperative for her peace of mind to devise an effective method of shutting of the sights. To avoid seeing her actions, to become blind to their meaning, to block insight into what they revealed was a vital demand.

In my next series of lectures I shall describe in detail how illusions are preserved by the expedient of looking away from actions. I shall then be able to demonstrate to you that such ludicrous and unworthy devices can be dispensed with if one learns to give up ludicrous and unworthy illusions. Margaret's tragedy was not that she looked away from her illusions; it was her tragedy that she entertained illusions which had to be looked away from. I once quoted the proverbial saying that "human nature cannot be changed," and commented on the absurdity and viciousness of the saying. Let me tell you that the "'human nature" that is here spoken of is nothing but the silly illusion of one's important or superior "self." That this illusion can be changed and that this sort of "human nature" can be disposed of I shall try to make clear to you in future discussions.

LECTURE 14

"FIRST SIGHT" AND "SECOND THOUGHT" IN TEMPER

You meet an old time friend on the street and are overjoyed at seeing him again after many years. You stroll with him exchanging recollections and reliving in memory experiences of the "good old days." On parting, you urge him to visit you at your home. "By the way. Charlie," you exclaim, "Why don't you come to dinner tonight?" Charlie accepts, and you saunter home, enjoying in advance the delights of being a host to your boyhood chum. Suddenly the thought strikes you that you should have consulted Louise, your wife, before making the engagement. She may not be prepared or may have made arrangements to visit her mother or to attend a club meeting. You now remember similar occasions when you brought home guests unexpectedly and caused Louise serious embarrassment. Your spirits drop. You realize that your ebullient temperament played you once again one of those tricks which place a heavy strain on domestic peace. Continuing your ruminations, you ponder your relationship to your wife. Of course, Louise has a right to resent your hasty decisions. She certainly has a right to be considered. But, after all, a husband has rights, too. And if an old chum turns up in town what is more natural than to have him as guest in your home? If Louise objects and raises a fuss well, there will be some commotion but she will have to realize that a husband has just as much right for consideration as a wife.

Arriving at home, you break the news to Louise with a sheepish smile and a voice trembling with uncertainty. Louise is perturbed, choking with indignation and struggling with tears. You try to calm her and advance

174

some clumsy remarks to the effect that, after all, the whole thing isn't worth arguing about and is it really so difficult to prepare another dish? Louise's face reddens; there is a stare of anger in her eyes. "Of course, it's nothing to you. All you are concerned about is your own comfort. My comfort counts for nothing. But let me tell you, I will not stand for any more insults. If you want to have Charlie here tonight I'll eat outside." The fight for which you prepared yourself when you indulged in your ruminations is now in full blaze, Louise contending for rightful consideration, you insisting on the wife's cooperation.

Actions Are "Looked At" From the Viewpoints of Either Personal Inclination or Impersonal Obligation

The account which I gave was one of behavior and action. You acted on your friend and on your wife. What was the meaning of the actions and how did you *look at* them? Clearly, before extending the invitation to the friend you were *disposed* to do so. Your disposition was that of friendship, jollity and good nature. The action which followed expressed your disposition and was prompted by it. I want you to understand this point: every action is preceded by a disposition.

Your disposition was at the same time an *inclination*. You extended the invitation because you were inclined to do so. I do not wish to give the impression that every disposition is in the nature of an inclination. This is by no means the case. If you scold your child you may do so from inclination but the chances are that you are not at all inclined to discipline your boy but feel you *have* to do it. In that case, your scolding is the result of an *obligation*. For some reason, you feel obliged to call your youngster to account although your paternal love and pride incline you to overlook the infantile misdemeanor. The example of the father will teach you that dispositions may be the result of either inclinations or obligations.

While speaking to your friend Charlie nothing was "in your mind" but your inclination to have a good time. After he left the thought of your wife struck you, and what entered your mind now was the obligation you had toward her. Now you looked at your action both from the viewpoint of inclination and that of obligation. You see here that *looking at* actions means to take a viewpoint. Pointing to the examples which I quoted I shall state that actions can be *looked at* or viewed from two viewpoints, either from the viewpoint of obligation or that of inclination.

Your inclination is your own and perhaps shared by nobody else. Right now while listening to this lecture you may feel inclined to contradict the statement which I just made. However, you may be the only one in this audience so inclined. Another listener may be so heartily in agreement with my view that he experiences the inclination to rise and cheer. Again, he too may be alone in his desire. Inclinations of this kind are purely *subjective and personal*. Your inclination to invite your friend Charlie was of this subjective and personal nature. Nobody in this world may have shared your disposition at that time; assuredly, your wife did not share it. Consider, in contrast, what is meant by obligations. You know that duty and responsibility oblige you to take into account the wishes and susceptibilities of your wife. However, it is not only you who has this obligation; everyone who is married has the same obligation with regard to his wife. Obligations are shared by all members of the group; they are not merely subjective and personal but, on he contrary, *objective and impersonal*. You will now understand that, in *looking* at your acts, you either take the subjective viewpoint of your personal inclination, or the objective viewpoint of your impersonal obligation.

We shall now return to Margaret and Tom whose

marital difficulties were discussed at considerable length. When Margaret harassed Tom with her unceasing complaints; when, wilfully and inconsiderately, she interfered with his business routine; when, from sheer whim and lust for domination, she forced him to forego the pleasures of ball games and hunting excursions; when finally in an almost fiendishly contrived caprice, she compelled him to transfer his morning shave from the privacy of the home to the publicity of the office; when all these inexcusable acts of a truly outrageous behavior were put into practice without the pretense of an apology or regret, we surmised that in order to preserve the illusion of her valuable "self" Margaret managed to blind herself to the meaning of her conduct. But how is this possible? Can anyone commit a cruel act and be blind to his cruelty? Margaret's behavior had all the earmarks of harshness and cruelty, and the obvious meaning of her reactions could not possibly escape her keen perception.

The Subjective Inclination Revealed by "First Sight" Is Justified, on "Second Thought" by the Claim of Objective Obligation

You will better understand what is meant by the terms "blinding oneself" to and *"looking away"* from the meaning of acts when you consider the simple example of a child being rudely disciplined by his father. The tot refuses to eat and is whipped for the presumed misdemeanor. What is the meaning of the father's behavior? If you question the boy he will not hesitate to inform you that father has a mean temper which inclines him to visit cruel punishment on his children. The mother will be more reticent and refrain from using condemnatory language but her anxious look and frantic plea for moderation will comfirm the boy's harsh opinion. She, too, thinks the father is cruel. Both place a charge against the father. They declare his act wrong, uncalled for and unjustified. On the other hand, the father places an entirely different construction on the matter. He will admit that, of course, the punishment was severe and, in a sense, cruel. Then he will exclaim in justification, "Can I help it? I tried kindness and persuasion and it didn't work. The boy is as stubborn as a mule. Much as I hate to use the strap I have to do it. I can't let my son grow up like a wild Indian." You see, son and mother *look at* the act and condemn it as the subjective inclination to be cruel. Father also *looks at* it as cruel but justifies it subsequently as an objective obligation. Father could express his position as follows: "At *first fight* my act may appear cruel and unjustifiable. But on *second thought,* it is clear that my seeming cruelty was justified by my obligation to punish the boy."

The distinction between first sight and second thought is basic for an understanding of temper. There is no father who, while caning or strapping his son, does not realize that his reaction is that of cruelty; there is no husband who, while berating his wife, is not aware of the pain he inflicts and the oppression he practices; and when Margaret tortured Tom with unreasonable requests and humiliating demands be certain that she was fully conscious of the fact that she played the role of the pitiless, implacable master who reduced Tom to a state of abject marital slavery. The calamity is that this state of affairs is recognized by father, husband, and wife at first sight only and that the *first sight glance* is speedily followed by a *second thought view.* What the first sight glance revealed as the father's cruelty, the husband's oppression and the wife's relentless craving for power is, on second thought, justified as necessity, duty or right. We then hear the father exclaim that, true, he was cruel but of necessity because the stubbornness of the boy forced him to be cruel; and the husband will hold forth that his wife's tendency to neglect her duties placed him under *obligation* to treat her severely; and Margaret was never at a loss to explain and justify the degrading servitude to which she reduced Tom on the basis of her being a sick woman having a *right* to demand the services of her husband. The technique of the procedure is clumsy an disingenuous but of a surprising simplicity: second thought plays a trick on first sight. What is first perceived as vice (cruelty, oppression and enslavement) is subsequently justified as virtue (necessity, obligation and right).

"*First Sight*" *Blackens Shining Escutcheon* *of* "*Self,*" "*Second Thought*" *Whitens It*

The significance of the terms "looking at" and "looking away" from the meaning of acts ought to be plain by now. Briefly, the temperamental person looks at his act at first sight and looks away from it by means of second thought. What he observes at first sight points disturbingly at his personal inclination. There he catches sight of his cruelty, oppressiveness or lust for power. The sight is shocking and discomforting; it challenges the value of his ego and threatens to weaken his sense of importance and to shake the foundations of his self-respect and self-confidence. The fond illusion of a valuable "self" is in jeopardy if the revelations of the first sight observations are permitted to go uncorrected. Correction of the first impression is imperative and conveniently supplied by the sophistry and specious arguments of second thought. By means of a clever trick the reprehensible nature of the personal inclination is admitted but justified as dictated by such impersonal qualities as necessity, duty, obligation. First sight blackens the shining escutcheon of the "self" but second thought hastens to whiten it by means of justification.

Margaret was a past master at the game of justifying cruel and oppressive inclinations into lofty and generous obligations. However, it was a game without a chance to win. In the end, she was invariably the loser. Outwardly she was successful and victorious in her endeavor to subdue Tom; but inwardly she was tense, nervous and irritable. There was never peace, hardly ever a fleeting truce in her life. Restlessness was the keynote of her existence. Repose and relaxation were denied her. Her tenseness deprived her of the fruits of victory; her nervousness prevented her from enjoying success. Why was she nervous, why tense?

In Temper Reprehensible Inclinations Are Justified as Creditable Obligations

Margaret was not alone in her inability to enjoy the victories scored on the battlefields of justification. This tragic fate she shared with every person endowed with a violent or aggressive temper. *Temper means to give way to represensible inclinations and to justify them as creditable obligations.**

The calamity is that the reprehensible inclination is brought to the notice of the temperamental person by the brief flash of first sight. True, the skillful whitewash of justification is instantly resorted to in the second thought argument. But the damage is done; the reprehensible inclination *was seen* in the momentary revelation of the first sight and tenseness is the result. The situation becomes increasingly aggravated by an unfortunate vicious cycle. The tenseness caused by the first sight observation calls imperatively for relief. And relief can be obtained through justification only. Unfortunately, the justifying argument is not convincing. The average person finds it difficult to believe that cruelty is an obligation and oppression a duty. The inability to believe makes for doubt and insecurity and creates renewed tenseness. This calls for increased justification with the inevitable deepening of doubt and insecurity. Tenseness again supervenes pressing for

---

*For simplicity sake, "necessity" and "duty" are here omitted from the definition of temper and "obligation" alone included.

ever-growing bursts of justification, and so forth in endless cycles of tenseness mobilizing justification, and justification releasing tenseness. There is no peace, no respite, no shred of a chance for relaxation.

*The Vicious Cycle of Tenseness Mobilizing Justification,
and Justification Releasing Tenseness Produced Panic*

Margaret was acutely aware of her tenseness. In time, she began to take alarm at her inability to relax. Her first suspicion was directed, naturally enough, against a physical ailment. In consequence of the continuous nervous strain to which she was subjected she developed so-called nervous symptoms: pressure sensations, feelings of fatigue and exhaustion, palpitations, sweats, aches and pains, itches and rashes. Some of the symptoms were strangely fleeting, attacking one part of the body, disappearing suddenly and soon reappearing in another part. Their very changeability and fitfulness mystified and terrified Margaret. She brooded, lost sleep, felt weary and miserable. The family physician was consulted and suggested the services of a specialist. Margaret was run through a series of physical examinations, X-ray studies and laboratory tests and was finally declared to be "in perfect physical health." Now her tenseness increased to intolerable proportions. She was gripped with the fear that she suffered from some mysterious sort of ailment that eluded diagnostic skill. The fear grew into panic; the panic aggravated the tenseness; the increased tenseness led to more frequent bursts of temperamental explosions. The vicious cycle of tenseness mobilizing justification and justification releasing tenseness was now perpetually in operation upsetting her balance and making life an endless series of torture for herself and Tom.

Today, Margaret is sitting in your midst, with Tom by her side, listening to my account of her past misbehavior. The fact that she is with us is sufficient evidence that her misbehavior is past. The additional fact that she gave willingly and joyfully permission to have her "case" discussed is proof positive that her attitude has undergone a radical change. She is no longer the capricious, self-willed home tyrant, no longer tense and aggressive, no longer continually exploding and continually justifying. Instead, she displays an average temper, with average sensitiveness and average reaction. There is peace at home and relaxation in her body and mind. How was this transformation effected?

Through Recovery, Inc. Margaret Learned to Avoid "Looking Away"
From the Revelations of "First Sight" Experiences

When Tom, in desperation, solicited the help of his physican, he was urged to attend Recovery, Inc. meetings. He did but was unable to induce Margaret to join him in his Recovery, Inc. endeavor. Unperturbed, he continued his journeys to meetings, classes and parties and became ever more convinced that if Margaret was to be cured it could only be done through Recovery, Inc. But Margaret was unapproachable. Vaguely and dimly she sensed that Recovery's emphasis on sincerity and fearless self-scrutiny might gravely disturb her delicately balanced system of rationalizations and justifications. When Tom, returning from a Sunday conference, discoursed on the theme of the lecture she returned a disdainful smile, heaped ridicule on his naive faith and, at times, worked herself up to the pitch of a tantrum. But the tantrums had little effect on Tom. In previous days Margaret's explosions used to terrify him; now, he viewed them with mingled feelings of mild annoyance and calm composure. His faith was naive, but his knowledge had matured. Tantrums were the current topic at the meetings which he visited. In group psychotherapy classes and in instruction courses they were analyzed in their proper light and exposed as purposeful, infantile and symbolic. With a clear vision he was now able to look through them as means of domination. When Margaret complained of her *killing* headaches he sympathized with her but evinced serious doubt about their *killing* quality. When she accused him of indifference to her intolerable suffering the accusation no longer jangled the soft chords of a tender conscience; he no longer rushed to console and apologize; he merely repeated the Recovery, Inc. maxim that the worst thing for a sufferer to do is to increase the suffering by the release of temper explosions. His calm and objective manner of reacting to Margaret's complaints had a salutary effect. Margaret felt instinctively that her grip on Tom was weakening; that her old methods of dominating him had lost their effectiveness. Her pure feminine intuition told her that she had to devise means of restoring her waning influence in order to strengthen her crumbling hold on Tom. She knew that this could not be accomplished unless she shared his interests. And if his main interests centered around Recovery, Inc. activities she had to take her due share. And so Margaret decided to join Recovery, Inc. She did so with reluctance, gloomily anticipating boredom and mental torture, but her sombre forebodings were pleasantly disappointed. Her first contact with Recovery, Inc. was the occasion of a gathering arranged by the South Side group. When she left she was strangely relaxed, her feelings softened and mellowed. She was now eager to attend group psychotherapy classes and Sunday conferences and a new world of thought was opened to her vision, reshaping her valuations and remodelling her attitudes. When, at group psychotherapy, she listened to interviews between the attending physicians and patients she was made to face in her mind the issues involved in temperamental behavior. The contrast between personal inclination and impersonal obligation, between subjective disposition and objective attitude, between first sight and second thought was stated and repeated, pertinently analyzed and forcefully emphasized. And spontaneously and unobtrusively impulses were retrained and ideas reoriented, and in the process Margaret learned painlessly how to look at the uncomplimentary revelations of *first sight experiences* and how to avoid looking away from them by means of *second thought justifications*. The success of the training is evidenced by the repose which she now possesses and the relaxation which she enjoys. Nothing can better illustrate the thoroughness of the teaching effect than the fact that she and Tom are today among us listening with serene detachment to the portrayal of their past marital woes and present conjugal happiness.

As concerns concepts and formulations, Lecture 14 offers little new in the line of definitions and interpretations. The central theme revolves around the effects of "first sight" and "second thought." The reader will justly object that this is merely a repetition of what was discussed elsewhere. The revelations of "first sight" were amply consilered in Lecture 7 under the heading of *Insight,* and the sophistry of "second thought" was adequately analyzed in Lecture 10 under the heading of *Rationalizing Self-Deception*. This is true and the contents of the present chapter are undoubtedly repetitious. However, repetition is no vice; indeed, it is a virtue, provided the reiterated concept is given a new terminology and illustrated with new examples.

LECTURE 15

THE WILL TO MISUNDERSTAND

When Margaret displayed a domineering disposition was she driven by emotion or guided by thought? If the answer be, as it should be, that both emotion and thought had their proportional share, the question arises: was the thought the preponderant influence or was emotion?

Emotional Imbalance Versus Intellectual Instability

Recently it has been the custom to explain behavior and misbehavior alike on the basis of emotion mainly or exclusively. Thought, reflection and intellectual processes in general are reduced to a secondary and rather evanescent role. Read, for instance, the average popular book on crime. The emphasis is almost exclusively on emotional conflicts as the primary cause of delinquency. You are told that the criminal is some sort of human machine that is driven on toward the anti-social career by a powerful wave of hatred, hostility and aggression. The wave is traced back by skillful interpretation to its feeble beginnings in early infancy when it was nothing but a trickle of immature antagonisms. The picture is that of lurid resentments lodging mysteriously in the tender organism of the child, fattening on environmental frustrations, gradually crowding to the surface and finally gaining expression in the criminal act. After reading this account you cannot help gaining the impression that the infantile resentments and grudges were never as much as touched by ideas, thoughts, teachings and principles.

The doctrine of the preponderance of emotion over intellect seems to pervade every province of modern thought. Juvenile problem behavior, adult "nervousness," marital maladjustment and perhaps every variety of normal and abnormal conduct are credited these days to what is called "emotional instability," "emotional imbalance" or "emotional conflicts."

The general run of parents, teachers and preachers do not seem to share the view that human conduct is primarily dominated by emotion. In their effort to influence behavior they still use the intellectual methods of imparting thoughts, concepts, principles and standards to those they wish to educate and elevate. Who holds the correct view? Those who educate children in actual practice? Or those who write about them in theory?

Emotion Drives Man, Intellect Guides Him

In a familiar simile, emotion is likened to the fuel which furnishes the driving power of the automobile while intellect is portrayed as playing the role of the man at the steering wheel. The comparison is by no means apt but may serve the purpose of a rough illustration. Without fuel the car would not move; without proper steering it would lose direction and miss its goal. What is more important? Motion and speed, or goal and direction? Thus phrased, the question is beside the point. If you are a contestant in an automobile race, goal and direction are important but power and speed alone will win the race. Conversely, if without being paricularly hurried, you wish to reach a certain destination, speed and power will avail you little if you take the wrong direction and miss the goal. In other words, what is more important in a given enterprise—fuel or steering, emotion or intellect—depends entirely or largely on the purpose which drives or guides you. Emotion drives, intellect guides. Is it true that human behavior, normal or abnormal, is mainly the result of blind, irrational drives with guidance, goal and direction relegated to a rather insignificant, secondary role?

It is difficult to speak of emotion with anything approaching authority. The laws governing the operations of intellect are fairly well known, thanks to the discoveries made by students of logic, philosophy and grammar. Investigation into the field of emotion was less successful. Emotions do not lend themselves readily to rational analysis. Their very nature and essence is that they are irrational. A few things, however, are tolerably well known about their qualities and effects. Of these, I shall try to give you a brief account.

Example of Feelings Maintained, Disturbed and Restored by Successively Changing Thoughts

In the evening, after dinner, you are seated on the couch with your wife, chatting and planning. Bob and Lois, your son and daughter, are attending a party in the neighborhood. Bob, 22, is to be married soon; Lois, 18, will graduate in a few weeks. Fate has been kind to you. With a steady position, a cozy home, a loyal wife and two lovely children, there is hardly anything to wish for. Your income is by no means excessive; it is just comfortable. Nevertheless, you can afford to plan for the purchase of an automobile and to contemplate a vacation trip to the country. All in all, you have a right to feel satisfied, composed and self-confident.

While you are chatting with your wife the telephone rings and you rise from the couch to answer the call. When you return your countenance has changed. You no longer look contented and relaxed. Instead, you seem to be apprehensive, worried, disconcerted. The reason for the change in your feelings is a message from a colleague who informed you that the firm by which you are employed is in financial difficulties. A host of upsetting thoughts float through your brain. Your plans will have to be readjusted, the automobile will have to wait, the vacation trip postponed, and the preparations for the son's wedding and the daughter's graduation will have to take a drastic cut in style and expense. It is a painful realization and your happiness is gone, your comfort disturbed and your confidence shaken. Prior to receiving the message you felt secure; now you are seized with a *sense of insecurity*.

You spend as hectic, sleepless night, tortured by visions of insecurity and poverty. In the morning you arise with your thoughts focused on a future of struggle and misfortune. When you arrive at work you are listless an despondent, oppressed by gloomy anticipations. Life seems futile, work meaningless.

In the afternoon notice arrives from the president of the corporation announcing that a reorganizion has been effected guaranteeing the continued operation of the plant. The employees are given assurance that no layoff is planned. Instantly, your spirits rise, your despair is swept aside. You feel secure again, resume your plans for automobile, vacation trip, wedding and graduation and feel once more satisfied, composed and self-confident.

Analysis of Example in Terms of Thought and Feeling

The example which I quoted at length seems to represent an unbroken sequence of dramatically changing feelings. However, on closer analysis, you will realize that your reactions cannot possibly be explained on feeling alone. You sat with your wife and were happy. That the happiness was a feeling can hardly be doubted. But a thought was in some way connected with it. You felt happy and at the same time thought you were secure. *The feeling of happiness* was linked to the *thought of security*. Which was first and which second, which cause and which effect is difficult to state. You may have felt happy because you thought you were secure. In this case the thought of security would have caused the feeling of happiness. On the other hand, the happy feeling might have caused a sense of security. Whatever may be the relationship the fact is that thought (of security) and feeling (of happiness) were closely interwoven.

In the second phase of your experience the telephone message arrived. It conveyed the idea (thought) that your position was in danger, and turned happiness into unhappiness. Here, the causal relation is clear: the thought of insecurity produced the feeling of unhappiness.

Next came the second message, emanating from the office of the president and announcing that your position was safe. Cause and effect are here again clearly defined: the thought of security reestablished the feeling of happiness.

Perhaps it was unnecessary to choose an elaborate example for the purpose of demonstrating that feelings are frequently dependent on and caused by thoughts. Simple, everyday occurrences would have served the same purpose. Your baby is sick, and, thinking of danger, you feel despondent. After the physician assures you (makes you think) that it is nothing but a gastric upset you instantly feel relieved. Again, the thought of insecurity (concerning the baby's condition) produced the feeling of despondency; the feeling disappeared when the physician changed your thought. Another example: you move along in a department store hemmed in by a milling crowd. Suddenly you notice that your little son is missing. Alarming thoughts race through your brain and cause the feeling of panicky fear. After a few minutes the youngster emerges by your side, and your panic is instantly dissolved. Again, a thought caused a feeling and another thought removed it.

"Pure" Feelings Have Little Influence on Average Adjustment

I do not wish to be misunderstood as suggesting that feelings are always irretrievably linked to thought. There are the well-known feelings of hunger, thirst and sex. That they may occur without being initiated, carried or even remotely influenced by thought processes can be safely assumed. The same is true of the situation in which one person falls in love with the other. Even if you maintain that the lover has his thoughts about his idol and, for instance, thinks of her as charming, angelic and divine; nevertheless, his thoughts are obviously secondary to the feeling. The exalted feeling produces lofty thoughts, not the reverse.

I mentioned hunger, thirst, sex and love as examples of so-called "pure" feelings which have little or no admixture of thought. I could have added the fears and joys of the baby which must be "pure" feelings as the baby can hardly be credited with what we call thought. Finally, I could have referred to the "pure" emotions aroused by the beauty and majesty of nature, which, if genuine and not sentimental, are obviously not dictated by thought. The list is impressive but insignificant from the viewpoint of average daily adjustment. And what we are interested in are the daily and hourly reactions of father to son, mother to daughter, husband to wife. In the average home, hunger and thirst are hardly likely to determine behavior. The average husband and wife are not expected to carry their original infatuation into the daily marital scene. And as concerns sex the situation is clear: if, as some maintain, sex exercises a powerful influence on average daily existence the effect is due to the *thought about sex* rather than to the sexual impulses as such. Aside from the exceptional instances of sex aberrations and sex delin-quencies, sex life in itself is not likely to result in abnormal behavior. It produces maladjustment only or mainly if it is linked to such thoughts as sin, guilt, disgrace, self-blame and self-contempt, expectation of punishment and anticipation of dire consequence to health. Again, you see how even here thought dominates feeling.

The Popular Explanation For Emotional
Instability Is Lack of Understanding

After this lengthy exposition let me revert to my original question: was Margaret's behavior driven by emotion (feeling) or guided by intellect (thought)? On the face of it her life with Tom seems to have been an endless series of clashes, conflicts and upheavals. How could such a vast amount of friction and dissension be determined by anything but emotion! When Margaret threw a tantrum, what else but an easily aroused emotionality could have caused the commotion? Try as we may, it seems we cannot escape the conclusion that her maladjustment was produced by what is called emotional instability. Yet, had you asked any of her friends or any of Tom's associates and employees, their dictum would have been tersely and simply that the two did not understand one another. The emotional turmoil would have been reduced to an intellectual element: lack of mutual understanding.

What precisely was it that Margaret failed to understand? When she harassed Tom she certainly knew (understood) that she caused him suffering. When she staged a tantrum she did not have to be told that her emotions were in poor control and her behavior off balance. All of this she understood. Moreover, she was keenly aware of the fact that she had made a mess of her life and occasionally confessed this realization. One day I intimated to her that Tom was in danger of a relapse unless domestic friction was avoided. I caught her in a soft mood and obtained a frank confession of her shortcomings. Finally she exclaimed, "What is wrong with me, I guess, is that I have no aim in life. Perhaps I need a new set of valuations." I have heard repeatedly statements of this kind from "nervous" patients. They knew, exactly like Margaret, that they failed of their objective, confessed in utter sincerity that they were disgusted with themselves and protested that what they needed was a new table of valuations and an absorbing aim in life. Yet, in spite of this evidence of an almost penetrating insight, friends and neighbors accused them of lack of understanding.

Superficial Versus Subtle Understanding

Obviously, there is more than one variety of understanding. Somebody speaks a sentence and you understand that it is a command or request or plain announcement of an objective fact. Understanding of this sort is superficial and the result of common school knowledge. When people speak of lack of understanding they have a more subtle variety in mind. And there is abundant subtlety in daily life to cause mountains of misunderstanding.

One day Tom retired to his room intent on working on accounts which had to be prepared for the morning. Before leaving the dining room he turned to Margaret, requesting her not to disturb him. He had hardly been sitting a few minutes when the door opened and Margaret inquired whether she could have the pencil on the table. Soon she appeared again, "Honey, are you really busy? I am so lonesome. Couldn't we chat for a while?" Tom pleaded the urgency of his work but Margaret coaxed and cajoled and when finally Tom succeeded in shoving her gently through the door he was far behind in his work schedule. All evening Margaret persisted in interrupting Tom's work, entering the room under every kind of pretense. Once it was the newspaper which, she "was sure" he had in his briefcase; then it was an inquiry about the telephone address of a friend or an entirely unnecessary reminder about a social engagement which, she was afraid, "honey" might have forgotten.

Disturbances of this kind were routine in the household. They happened when Tom seated himself comfortably to read the evening paper and Margaret chose precisely this occasion to ask his help in lifing a package to the upper shelf of the pantry. The interference became almost unbearable when Tom was closeted with his bookkeeper and the radio was set going full blast in the adjoining room drowning conversation in a blare of noise. I could finish an almost endless list of similar instances of petty misbehavior, but the pattern would merely repeat itself.

Temperamental Persons Are Impelled by the Will to Misunderstand

Understanding is the *will to understand* but temperamental persons are impelled by the *will to misunderstand*. The misunderstandings furnish them the reasons and excuses for practicing their temper. The classical example is the husband who goes into a rage because dinner is not ready the moment he enters the home. If this enraged husband had the will to understand he would not have to dig deep to find the reason for the delay. He would easily understand, without effort of thought or special inquiry, that domestic affairs are never expected to run to schedule. He could discern by a mere flicker of reflection that a wife is frequently handicapped by the necessity of caring for the children, by an occasional defect in the gas range, by the failure of the grocer to deliver in time, by something going wrong in the preparation of the food, or by unexpected visitors dropping in at an inopportune moment. To understand all these possibilities requires nothing but the will to understand. If the husband fails to consider the possibilities be certain he is guided by nothing but the will to misunderstand.

With a Vast Capacity for Understanding Others Margaret Had the Will to Misunderstand Tom

I told you that Margaret's friends and Tom's associates ascribed the marital woes of the couple to a lack of

understanding. The phrase is incorrect. There is no such
thing as lack of understanding among adult persons who
belong to approximately the same social and educational
group. It does not require a super mind to analyze properly
the meaning of those "trifles and trivialities" which lead to
temperamental outbursts. Margaret had perfect understanding for the sensibilities and idiosyncrasies of those she
met at social funcitons. She was friendly to grocer,
butcher, scrub woman and window washer, and with the
neighbors she enjoyed the reputation of being a
sympathetic and understanding person. With so much
capacity to understand she could not possibly be charged
with lack of understanding, and if she currently
misunderstood Tom the only reason imaginable was the
will to misunderstand.

Goal Ideas and Pattern Ideas

A will is a feeling linked to a so-called goal idea. You
have here again a combination of a feeling joined to a
thought. I shall try to explain to you what is meant by the
term "goal idea." This house which you see through the
window gives rise to the idea of a brick structure rising five
stories above the ground, being topped by a flat roof and
having a clean appearance. What is here described is all
form and pattern. The thought which went through your
mind at the sight of the house may, therefore, be called a
form idea or a pattern idea. You do not own the house, nor
do you wish to buy it,, nor do you occupy a room or
apartment in it. This being the case, the house does not
represent any goal to you. Should you intend to acquire the
property, or to live in it, the house would be related to you
as a goal, and the thought of the house would be one of
your *goal ideas*.

A mother possesses form and pattern but has, in the
main, the status of a goal. Your goal is to please her, to
consider her comfort and welfare, to sacrifice time and

effort in her behalf. If linked to a strong feeling of love the goal idea creates the will to be a devoted son. Similarly, your craving (feeling) for privacy and security, linked to the goal idea of a home, may create the will to buy a house. These examples, I think, will illustrate to you what is meant by a goal idea, and you will now understand what I intended to express when I said that a will is a feeling linked to a goal idea.

Will to Peace as Opposed to Will to Power

In a group (marriage, friendship, business partnership) there are two principal goal ideas: cooperation or competition, mutuality or rivalry. The feeling of fellowship linked to the goal ideas of cooperation and mutuality, gives rise to the *will to peace*. The feeling of self-importance, linked to the goal ideas of competition or rivalry, yields the *will to power*. The will to peace makes for understanding, the will to power for misunderstanding.

When months ago I discussed the development of the normal child I painted the picture of an unbounded will to power. Power means many things to the child. It means, for instance, demanding a piggy-back ride precisely at the moment when father is busy with an important task; it means yelling, sulking and whining if the ride is denied, or insistence on repetition after repetition if it is granted. Power also means resisting being put to bed or, once in bed, complaining that the blanket is too warm and making mother change it, asking for a drink of water and making mother bring it, discovering a fanciful cold and asking mother to fetch a handkerchief. Add the subsequent demand to "get the other doll" and the plea that mother stay with the tot "just a little while," and the infantile will to power is adequately characterized as that tendency which secures satisfaction at the expense of others' discomfort.

Children Have Lack of Understanding, Adults Have Will to Misunderstand

In a child you expect reactions of this kind and excuse them on the grounds that intellect is in its infancy and knowledge has not ripened. Let the child break china or make a vicious pass at other children and the mother, even if she gives him a spanking, will, nevertheless, excuse the youngster because he is "just a child that doesn't know what he is doing." You see, in the child the will to power is or may be linked to a "lack of understanding." But, mark it, in the child only. There, one actually gains the impression that some children at least are naughty without being aware of their naughtiness. That adult persons should engage in a persistent course of demanding, opposing, stalling and obstructing without the knowledge that their behavior is offending against rules and disturbing peace can hardly be assumed. You may take it for granted that if an adult person exercises the will to power he does so from a will to misunderstand, not from a lack of understanding.

The average person is born with the will to power and acquires, through education, the will to peace. As the child passes through adolescence to maturity the will to peace takes the lead over the will to power. This is accomplished by the influence of home, school, church and other educational forces. What the educators do is to make the child adopt the adult goal ideas of cooperation and mutuality and to crowd back the infantile goal ideas of competition and rivalry. After imbibing the adult goal ideas the individual establishes the will to peace and the corresponding will to understand. An education of his kind presupposes that intellect (goal ideas) has the power to curb or release socially undesirable feelings, emotions and impulses. If guided by peace ideas they are curbed, if driven on by power ideas they are currently released.

Margaret's Re-education Was Effected through Influencing Her Goal Ideas

As concerns the acquisition of adult goal ideas, education miscarried in the case of Margaret. After reaching adulthood she still maintained an immoderate will to power and an implacable will to misunderstand. This was true, however, of her marital relations only. As friend, hostess, guest and customer she was courteous and accommodating and not at all impelled by a drive for power. Even in her marital life, moreover, she was frequently sweet and sympathetic, considerate and affectionate. In this manner she was at the same time driven by the will to power and guided by the will to peace. Margaret was sufficiently sophisticated and introspective to be aware of the clash of the two wills. She sensed the implied contradiction when she practiced infantile goal ideas with Tom and adult goal ideas with others. The contradiction confused her and weakened her self-assurance. As a result, her self-regard suffered. She pertinently analyzed her sorry plight when she confessed that she had no aim in life and needed a new set of valuations. Of course, the analysis was half correct only. It was not true that she had no aim; the truth was that she had two contradictory aims (power and peace) and was guided by two mutually exclusive goal ideas (mutuality and rivalry). In consequence of this duality of wills and goal ideas her behavior gave the appearance of conflicting, ill balanced and unstable action. I hope you will now realize that her difficulties were less in the sphere of emotions than in that of intellect and that what appeared to be "emotional conflicts," "emotional imbalance," and "emotional instability" should preferably be called "intellectual conflicts," "intellectual imbalance" and "intellectual instability." Let me add in conclusion that when Margaret joined Recovery, Inc. and underwent a process of reeducation it was not so much her emotions which were reeducated as it was the more intellectual functions of will and goal ideas.